Penguin Books
Before the Revolution

Kyril FitzLyon is Russian by origin (his Russian name is
Kyril Zinovieff), but came to England as a child in 1920.
He served in the army during the war, and immediately
after it joined the Ministry of Defence. He has translated
and edited a number of Russian and French writers,
including Dostoyevsky, Paustovsky, and Sinyavsky. His
reviews of books on Russian and other subjects have
appeared in the *Daily Telegraph*, *The Times Literary
Supplement*, *London Magazine* and other periodicals.

Tatiana Browning, who collected the photographs, is half-
Russian. She has worked for a number of years as a picture
researcher for publishers, specializing in Russian and
Eastern art.

KYRIL FITZLYON AND TATIANA BROWNING

BEFORE THE REVOLUTION

A View of Russia under the Last Tsar

PENGUIN BOOKS

PENGUIN BOOKS

Published by the Penguin Group
27 Wrights Lane, London W8 5TZ, England
Penguin Books USA Inc., 375 Hudson Street, New York, New York 10014, USA
Penguin Books Australia Ltd, Ringwood, Victoria, Australia
Penguin Books Canada Ltd, 10 Alcorn Avenue, Toronto, Ontario, Canada M4V 3B2
Penguin Books (NZ) Ltd, 182–190 Wairau Road, Auckland 10, New Zealand

Penguin Books Ltd, Registered Offices: Harmondsworth, Middlesex, England

First published by Allen Lane 1977
Published in Penguin Books 1982
Reprinted with a new preface 1992
10 9 8 7 6 5 4 3 2 1

Made and printed in Great Britain by
Butler & Tanner Ltd, Frome and London

Set in Monophoto Photina

Preface to the Allen Lane Edition

It is best to start by stating the obvious: this is a book of photographs. In other words, it is haphazard, it is self-indulgent, it is patchy. It is also, I hope, evocative. It may, in a sense, be history, but it is not a history book. It evokes a past which is not very distant. After all, many of the men and women in these photographs, though they must remain anonymous, are still very much with us, still carrying on with their lives, even if in another, entirely different, environment from that in which they are shown here. And yet, for all its relative nearness, it is a past which seems immensely far away. For what it reflects is a society which has no links with the present. Unlike, say, English or French society, which has not broken with its past, but has evolved from it.

In fact, what these photographs evoke is Atlantis. Atlantis-fashion, suddenly, totally and irrevocably, perhaps undeservedly (though not inexplicably), the world they immobilize suddenly sank and disappeared from view – its culture vigorous and intact, its economy in full, indeed unprecedented, development, many of its most cherished political and social goals either realized or well within reach. The men and women who inhabited it are like the people in Hilaire Belloc's verses, who

> . . . married and gave in marriage,
> And danced at the County Ball,
> And some of them had a carriage,
> And the flood destroyed them all.

Only the photographs remain, the flotsam and jetsam of an immense shipwreck, each perpetuating a moment of time, a society and a way of life gone beyond recall.

However, photographs can only reproduce the likeness of tangible reality, objects animate and inanimate. Through these they can, if they are good, not merely illustrate events – they can illuminate them. They can also give visible form to habits and customs which make up a way of life. They cannot interpret events or explain the reasons which made men adopt certain views and reject others. They can only indicate the physical framework within which these men operated. Photographs, in short, show the world as it is (or was) and not as it should be (or should have been).

The text serves merely as an introduction to the photographs, and since an introduction is limited by what it introduces, I have avoided the discussion of the all-important political, economic, military, and other issues that shook the Russian Imperial regime to its foundations and, in the end, caused its dramatic collapse. I have merely tried to deal with the social framework – since this is what these photographs illustrate – within which these issues had their validity. Thus, since some photographs are of men and women belonging to the many minorities inhabiting the Russian Empire, I felt I had at least to touch upon the way in which those minorities lived, how many of them there were, what the Russian attitude to them was and how Russians – ordinary Russians, peasants – reacted to the great empty spaces which they found beyond the Urals.

Similarly, photographs of peasants caused me to deal with the physical aspect of Russian villages and of the houses in them, the everyday life of their inhabitants and the particular (and peculiar) type of land tenure which circumscribed the life of Russian peasants. The same, *mutatis mutandis*, with the life of the gentry or of the urban working classes or of the Imperial family. This kind of approach led me to deal with the latter by describing the routine of the Emperor's and Empress's social life and their reaction to it, and to examine their financial situation – this last, because it is so seldom mentioned except to say, incorrectly, that the Emperor was the richest man in the world.

The period spanned by the photographs (and introduction) is the last quarter of a century of the Russian, as distinct from the Soviet, Empire. In order to set a precise date to the beginning of this period, the year chosen as point of departure was 1894 – by no means an arbitrary date.

Politically, it was the year of the last Emperor's accession to the throne. In a monarchical country, which was also an autocracy, this was a key factor. The personality of the autocrat was bound to influence the course and character of events. It did. For one thing he ceased to be an autocrat. The change from autocracy to a constitutional (or semi-constitutional) form of government followed on a defeat in war and a revolution (the war with Japan and the revolution of 1905), and involved the country in a political and social struggle which permeated directly or indirectly almost every national activity. The struggle did not abate even during the First World War and ended with the Emperor's abdication and the monarchy's collapse – only to continue against another form of autocracy. This time, however, it was the autocracy that emerged victorious – but that takes us outside our set period.

Economically, too, the starting date seems to me fairly suitable since the early 1890s witnessed a turn in the policy of industrialization and an upsurge of economic development, which produced and then exceeded an eight per cent annual rise in industrial production, far above anything reached in other major European countries at the time. A recession which followed the boom in 1900 proved purely temporary, and in the decade between the first revolution in 1905 and the First World War in 1914 industrial output again rose at an impressive average annual rate of six per cent. This may have been slightly lower than in the 1890s, but it was accompanied – as the 1890s boom had not been – by an expansion of agricultural production and a rise in peasant prosperity. It was, it is true, a very inadequate rise and a very inadequate prosperity: the peasants, generally speaking, remained abysmally poor. However, a really radical improvement in their lot seemed to be in the offing, brought about mainly by the government's agrarian reforms. These aimed at turning the peasants' strips of cultivated land, communally held, into consolidated farms in individual ownership and, therefore, turning the peasants themselves into farmers, at transferring State and much of the Imperial family's and landowners' land to peasant ownership by facilitating its purchase by peasants, at opening up empty Siberian acres to land-hungry Russian peasants and at providing them with capital and with agricultural machinery. In Lenin's view expressed at the time, these reforms, particularly those abolishing the commune and creating a farmer class in place of the peasant, were nothing less than 'revolutionary'. But alas, they were, he thought, capable of competing all too successfully with his own plans and, therefore, making his own revolution difficult to achieve. For if allowed to continue, the Russian government's policy would, he said, force him and his party 'to give up any agricultural policy programme in a bourgeois society'.

Educationally, the 1890s witnessed the beginning of a new policy, though its real development and a more radical spread of education came a little later – at the turn, and in the early years of the twentieth century.

Finally, literature and the arts. The emergence of the World of Art movement in the early 1890s and of the Moscow Art Theatre shortly after, the first appearance of Symbolist and other literary currents which were to lift Russian literature out of the doldrums, all combine to make the 1890s the watershed they proved to be in so many other aspects of national activity in Russia.

Perhaps I should add one last point to this catalogue of reasons for choosing the 1890s as a starting point. The first Russian Population Census was taken in January 1897, and a vast amount of social, economic and other information came to light, providing a point of reference and comparison which would not have otherwise been available. Henceforth, the mid 1890s became a firm basis for the analysis of Russia's development in the last quarter of a century of its existence – until, that is, it turned into the U.S.S.R.

Preface to the 1992 Reprint

Since *Before the Revolution* was first published in 1977 fundamental, indeed dramatic, changes have taken (and are still taking) place on the territory of the former Soviet Union. Its very name has disappeared from the map along with the Communist Party which ruled it throughout its existence to the exclusion of all other political organizations. The new entity that has replaced the USSR – the Commonwealth of Independent States (CIS) – does not, since the secession of the Baltic republics, cover quite the same area, and its very survival, at least in its present form, is in considerable doubt.

For obvious reasons, however, none of this can alter or invalidate anything I have written in my preface to a book dealing with events and a social scene dating back to the turn of the turn of the present century. Nevertheless, were I to write it now, I would be tempted to make certain observations which would have been quite inapplicable fifteen years ago.

I would consider it appropriate, for instance, when mentioning Russia's rapid economic development under capitalism in the twenty or so years preceding the Communist Revolution (p. 8) to point out that the failure of the system adopted after the Revolution is leading Russia's present rulers to abandon Marxism and revert to a market economy.

Similarly, when mentioning Lenin's hostile attitude to Stolypin's agricultural reforms (pp. 8 and 30) it would be relevant to mention the current tendency to rehabilitate those reforms. I would probably balance my remarks regarding the abolition by the Soviet government of private property in land and peasant land tenure (p. 30) by a reference to the recent tentative (and to date not very effective) legislation aiming at the restoration of private farming.

In this connection, and in describing land-owners' country estates such as they existed prior to the Revolution (p. 24), I would probably indicate the welcome now sometimes extended to those landowners' descendants on a visit to their families' former estates from their West European or American exile and to the offer

occasionally, though unofficially, made to restore to them their ancestral home.

Again, when speaking of the Russian monarchy's collapse and disappearance (p. 19), the current revival of Russian interest in the institution itself as well as in the fate of the last monarch and his family could be noted, as well as a growing sympathy for, and a deeper understanding of, the difficulties he had to contend with in confronting the events of his reign.

In the sphere of literature and the arts (pp. 58–65) it would be equally appropriate to comment on the current trend towards a greater appreciation of Russian early twentieth-century achievements, and on the frequently expressed regret at the cultural loss suffered by Russia after 1917 as the result of both the emigration of writers and the persecution and suicide of so many who remained in the USSR (p. 66).

The extraordinary reversal of political, economic and social policies amounts in fact to a revolution, but a revolution for which the appropriate slogan should be: 'Forward into the past!' It is a revolution which looking for suitable symbols finds them in the restoration of pre-1917 emblems. The old Russian Tricolour has taken the place of the Red Flag, and the Double-headed Eagle has been proposed instead of the Hammer-and-Sickle. Russia has jettisoned its title as the RSFSR, and pre-1917 names have been readopted for cities, streets and institutions that had commemorated post-1917 heroes and events.

How far all these changes, whether fundamental or superficial, will go, or how permanent they will prove to be, it is as yet too early to say. It is of course obvious that, however favourably the pre-Revolutionary past may come to be regarded, the restoration of that past in any meaningful sense is not a possibility which can be seriously contemplated. For that reason the picture of the Russian pre-Revolutionary society which I have tried to draw in my introduction and which is conveyed (I hope) by the photographs will continue to reflect an unrepeatable moment in time, an Atlantis (whatever its qualities and defects) gone beyond recall. This new printing, therefore, carries the text of the old in its entirety, except for the passage referring to the Romanov Dynasty's *legitimist* right to the Russian Crown (p. 17). The death of Prince (generally, though erroneously, styled 'Grand Duke') Vladimir of Russia in April 1992 has meant that all members of the Romanov Dynasty now living are descendants of morganatic marriages. Since these are excluded from the right of succession to the Russian throne by the laws introduced in the nineteenth and early twentieth centuries by the then reign-ing Russian emperors, the Dynasty can be said to have legislated itself out of the right of succession – a curious and unforeseen consequence of Imperial legislation.

When the Russian version of my introduction appeared in 1983 it had to be smuggled into the Soviet Union in order to circumvent censorship. It is a measure of the change in Russia's political circumstances and climate, and of the triumph of *glasnost*, that now, of course, it is freely available in Russia both in bookshops and in libraries.

K. F.
1992

Acknowledgements

We are particularly grateful to Monsieur V. Bellin for his generous assistance with the picture research in Paris.

In the following list of acknowledgements for the pictures the reference numbers given are those of pages; where there is more than one photograph on a page, the pictures are identified as a, b, c, starting from the top of the page.

Anglican and Eastern Churches Association, 110a, 111a, 136b, 170, 171b; Archives of the Museum of the Russian Military Past, Paris, 85a, 85b, 94, 95a, 96a, 96b, 97, 98, 99a, 101, 102a, 105a, 106b, 164b, 203; Mme von Bader, 159a; Mr A. Bakhroushin, 60, 160a; Bibliothèque Nationale, Paris, 124a, 127a, 167; Mrs J. M. Bielak, 128a, 141b, 168, 173b, 178b, 180a, 183, 192a; Bildarchiv Foto Marburg, 110b, 185c; Countess O. Bobrinskoy, 194b; Mr Leo Bothas, 74b, 80b, 84b, 89a, 93b, 112a, 163b; B.B.C. Archives, 201b; Mrs Caird Levitsky, 192b; Mrs T. Carson, 161, 165a; Mrs V. Dixon, 83a, 91, 93a; Mrs A. Dryden, 108b, 109, 128b, 162; Mrs M. Dunlop, 89b; Éditeurs Réunis, Paris, 82, 137b, 138a, 139, 141a, 143; Mr N. Eselenov, 140, 175; Mrs E. Fabri, 130, 131a, 131b; Mr K. FitzLyon, 160b; Foyer des Anciens Officiers Russes, Paris, 99b, 100b; Princess N. Galitzine, 90a, 113b, 136a, 137a, 138b; Mr R. Garnett, 116b, 120, 121a, 121b, 122a, 122b, 123a, 123b; Mr H. H. Goodwin, 155, 194a, 201a; The Gramophone Co. Ltd, Hayes, 200; the Kodak Museum, Harrow, 151a, 151b; Mr Jonathan Lewis, 76a, 76b; Pierre Matisse Gallery, New York, 63; Baroness G. von Meck, 88a–d, 166a; Musée de l'Homme, Paris, 27, 39, 47, 118a, 119, 126, 129a, 177, 184, 189a, 189b, 190, 191a; Musée du Régiment des Cossaques de la Garde Impériale, Paris, 118c, 129b, 158, 159b; Mr A. Neville, 72b, 74a, 75, 77; Novosti, 31, 55, 100a, 108a, 134, 135b, 144a, 148, 152a, 152b, 157, 196, 197a, 198a, 199; Paul Popper Ltd, London, 42, 80a, 105b, 107, 113a, 144b, 146, 153, 154b, 156, 164a, 169; Pavlova Museum, London, 197b, 198b; Private Collection, London, 92b, 132a, 132b, 133; Reproduced by Gracious Permission of H.M. The Queen, 14, 73, 81b; Roger-Viollet, 34, 79b, 81a, 83b, 103, 114, 193, 195; Royal Geographical Society, 111b, 112b, 117, 176b, 182a, 182b, 185a, 185b; School of Slavonic and East European Studies, London, 20, 86a, 86b, 87, 163c, 165b, 166b; Shell Library, London, 135a; Somoff Collection, 72a; Staatsbibliothek, Berlin, 115a, 145; the late Lady Studd, 84a; Ullstein GMBH Bilderdienst, 102b; Victoria and Albert Museum, 51, 71, 79a, 106a, 115b, 116a, 118b, 124b, 125, 127b, 142, 149, 171a, 173a, 174a, 174b, 176a, 178a, 179, 180b, 181a–d, 186, 187a, 187b, 188, 191b; Mr I. Vinogradov, 95b; Mr N. Volkow-Mouromtzov, 78, 154a; Wartski, London, 150; Mrs E. Zinovieff, 90b, 92a, 104, 163a, 172.

'. . . and the flood destroyed them all'

HILAIRE BELLOC

Tsar Nicholas II (1868–1918) reading the Peterburgskiye Vedomosti *(Petersburg News), the official gazette.*
An informal study from the royal albums at Windsor.

Russian Society in the Reign of Nicholas II

'What am I going to do? What is going to happen to me . . . to all of Russia? I am not prepared to be a Tsar. I never wanted to become one.' These words were addressed to his brother-in-law by a young man of twenty-six, in tears at the realization that now his father was dead he had become the Emperor of Russia.

Nicholas II may not have broken his customary reserve to quite the extent his brother-in-law alleges, but no doubt that was how he felt, for that October evening in 1894, a few hours after the Emperor Alexander III's death, he wrote despairingly in his Diary: 'Lord, help us in these grim days!' Weeks went by, and the despair, the near-panic, obviously subsided. Two months later, on New Year's Eve, he could confide to his Diary that he was looking into the future 'without fear', but he still referred to his father's death and his own accession to the throne as 'the worst thing that could have happened to me, the thing I had been dreading so much all my life'.

But that was not what this outwardly calm, undemonstrative man, with his iron self-control, which so disconcerted his more exuberant subjects, allowed the world to see. For in the world's eyes, Nicholas was the mightiest monarch on earth, who not only had no limits to his rights and prerogatives other than those set by international obligations and his own conscience, but who combined absolute power with sway over one-sixth of the planet's surface. When his titles, emphasizing the vastness of his dominions, were read out in the course of his coronation, he was hailed as the Emperor and Autocrat of all Russia, as well as (somewhat superfluously, one would have thought) of Moscow, Kiev, Vladimir and Novgorod; Tsar, too, of course, though not of Russia, but of Kazan, Astrakhan, Poland, Siberia, Khersones, and Georgia — in that order. Of his other dominions and provinces he was either Prince (as of Estonia), Grand-Duke (as of Finland and Lithuania) or Sovereign (as of Pskov, Turkestan and 'the Armenian Regions'). He was also 'Lord and Master of All Northern Countries' — an ambitious, if vague, title — as well as Duke of territories outside his control, such as Schleswig-Holstein and Oldenburg, and 'Heir of Norway', a claim of little practical significance. These strange historical claims take long to die. It was only in the last century that British monarchs ceased to style themselves Kings of France.

In the concept of both Tsar and Emperor the secular was fused with the spiritual. Immediately after the Coronation — when the Emperor placed the crown upon his own head — for no-one else was deemed worthy of doing so — he was, for the only time in his life, admitted into the Sanctuary to receive the Sacraments in accordance with a rite reserved for priests alone.

Since the days of Peter the Great in the eighteenth century, it could be argued that a Russian Empress was associated with her husband as co-ruler rather than merely as Consort, and the Empress Alexandra, writing to Nicholas in the first person plural: 'We have been placed by God on a throne', had some theoretical justification. For, like him, and unlike a Queen Consort in any other country, she was crowned with the Crown of State (symbolically: the Emperor merely touched her forehead with it), and like him, she was anointed, though not with full rites.

The Coronation ceremony took place, as tradition demanded, in Moscow's Cathedral of the Assumption. It was followed by a huge banquet for seven thousand guests, from which all foreigners were excluded, even ambassadors and foreign princes. They were, however, allowed to watch the scene from a gallery reserved, in the days before Peter the Great, for Royal ladies, who could not then take part in public ceremonies, but could watch them, properly concealed behind a screen. In the vast crowd of officials, ministers of State, Court functionaries, church dignitaries, Service officers, special envoys of Russia's numerous minorities, etc., all in resplendent uniforms, vestments and national dress, there was one group of people in ordinary, if Sunday-best, clothes, who were present by hereditary right. They were the descendants of those who had, at any time in history, saved the life of a Russian sovereign. Prominent among them were the descendants of Ivan Susanin (opera lovers will remember the hero of Glinka's opera). He had been tortured and killed by Russia's Polish invaders in the seventeenth century, for refusing to reveal the hiding place of Michael, the first Tsar of the Romanov Dynasty. Now, some three centuries later, Susanin's descendants, peasants as he himself had been, were feasting at the Coronation banquet of the Dynasty's last Tsar.

But the festivities, the pomp and circumstance, all turned to disaster, which was interpreted as a bad omen for the future and cast its shadow over the whole reign. Three days after the Coronation, an enormous crowd of about half a million had assembled on the Khodynskoye Polye — now an airfield — just outside Moscow, waiting for the expected distribution of free beer and mementoes. The density of the crowd caused accidents, mainly from suffocation, the accidents resulted in a panic, and, in the general stampede, great numbers of people were injured or crushed to death. The Emperor's first impulse, to go into a retreat for a few days in token of national mourning, was thwarted by incompetent advice tendered to him by his uncles of whom he stood in awe. It was particularly urged on him that a refusal to attend the ball given that night by the French ambassador would be misinterpreted by the French government as a diplomatic insult. Too inexperienced to ignore the pressure put upon him, Nicholas complied with the advice and thereby earned for himself a reputation for callousness which pursued him relentlessly for ever more and is still a frequent cliché. It was one of the government's many mistakes, magnified and often distorted by hostile propaganda, which an efficient Public Relations Office, had one existed, would have helped to avoid. On this occasion, gifts of money to victims and their relatives out of Imperial family funds produced no effect on the chorus of bitter vituperation, which tended to obscure the fact that the accident was, after all, an accident and not a gruesome act committed purposely by the authorities.

Inevitably, life at the Russian Court, like life at any Court, was artificial in the sense that it was governed by tradition and ceremonial. Individual Tsars tried to escape by fencing off their private life as much as possible from their public functions. Nicholas's exceptional reserve and his wife's painful shyness, together with the greatly in-

creased security precautions introduced after Alexander II's assassination in 1881, isolated the Imperial couple from the country and the society in which they lived to a degree never witnessed in Russia before. Gone were the days when the sovereign and his wife would drop in on friends in their homes or would be seen walking in St Petersburg's public park (the Summer Garden), or mix with the crowd in the streets. Apart from occasional visits to the Winter Palace for the performance of some State or social function, Nicholas and Alexandra avoided the Capital as much as they could and spent most of the year in near-by Tsarskoye Selo. There they lived in the Alexander Palace, occupying its private apartments, decorated and furnished to resemble an English country house. These apartments were guarded against the intrusion of the outside world by four gigantic 'Ethiopians', as they were known at Court — in fact, three Abyssinians and one American Negro — in white turbans, baggy red breeches, black, gold-embroidered jackets and yellow shoes, curving upwards at the toes (a costume which cannot help reminding the modern reader of the Moor in the ballet 'Petroushka'). Their duties were limited to opening and closing doors and to intimating 'by a sudden noiseless entrance into a room', as one witness puts it, 'that one of their Majesties was about to appear'.

After a winter spent in Tsarskoye Selo, the Imperial family would move for a few weeks to neighbouring Peterhof, founded by Peter the Great in the eighteenth century in emulation of Versailles. A cruise in the yacht *Shtandart* was sometimes undertaken in early summer, and later the family might visit Poland, staying in a hunting lodge in Spala. Finally, in the autumn they would go for a short spell to Livadia, their estate in the Crimea. The large timber house which stood in a magnificent park and in which Nicholas's father, Alexander III, had died, was pulled down in Nicholas's reign and a gleaming white palace overlooking the sea, was built in its stead. But it was finished only about three years before the war and the family did not have time to enjoy it for very long. After that, back again to Tsarskoye Selo.

Disliking 'Society' herself, Alexandra preferred her children to have as little to do with it as possible. As a result, they very seldom saw anyone of their own age, except their first cousins, and even that was rare. Alexandra was painfully aware of her own unpopularity, which was probably partly due to her stiff bearing and introspective nature interpreted as haughtiness, but which she took for disloyalty to herself and particularly to her husband. She shared with him the conviction that true monarchist feeling (equated by her with patriotism) was to be found among 'the people', the peasants, and not among either intellectuals or politicians or the upper classes – none of them qualifying, in her mind, as genuinely Russian. It was this conviction, sincerely held by them both, that underlay the Emperor's failure to come to terms with the central issue of his reign – the constitutional regime thrust upon him, he considered, by 'un-Russian' elements (understood in a way which makes this expression in many respects comparable to the term 'un-American' – un-American activities – as it came to be used in the United States half a century later).

Socially, this attitude led to an isolation which caused the Imperial couple to see few people beyond those they saw *ex officio*: foreign ambassadors, ministers of State, senior civil servants and Service officers, Court officials, ladies-in-waiting, A.D.C.s etc. and, of course, members of the, admittedly enormous, Romanov clan. The Empress's friendship for Anna Vyroubova, who held no official post, was quite exceptional. Her relationship to Rasputin was based on his reputed healing powers, which he exercised to cure her son whenever his haemophilia resulted in haemorrhages. Besides, both Nicholas and Alexandra had the impression that in talking to Rasputin they were dealing with a true Russian peasant, a real 'man of the people', which he certainly was. To them he represented a direct link with 'the people', which 'Society', ladies-in-waiting, Court officials, and ministers equally certainly did not.

The 'enormous Romanov clan' consisted, apart from Nicholas, Alexandra and their five children, of the Dowager Empress, a score of grand-dukes (sons and grandsons of a Russian sovereign), rather fewer grand-duchesses and a dozen or so princes and princesses 'of Imperial Blood' – a Russian sovereign's great-grand-children: some sixty individuals altogether. The

Russian Law of Succession allowed no grand-duke or grand-duchess to contract a morganatic marriage – to marry, that is, outside the circle of reigning European dynasties. The consent of the Emperor was, in any case, obligatory. The penalty for transgressing that law was the exclusion certainly of the transgressor's children and possibly (the law was not clear on this point) of the transgressor himself (or herself) from the line of succession to the throne. The same penalties were imposed on princes and princesses of Imperial Blood who married morganatically, though in their case the marriages themselves were not (after 1911) forbidden by law. In practice the prohibition to marry commoners was largely disregarded (as was the obligation to ask the Emperor's permission), with the result that within the Emperor's immediate family, two out of his three siblings – a brother and a sister – were married to commoners and only one of his male first cousins married royalty. (It may be of some academic interest to note that since all the Romanovs at present living are descendants of morganatic marriages, no member of the Romanov family can have a *legitimist* claim to the throne of Russia.)

The outward pomp and circumstance surrounding the public appearances of the Emperor and Empress gave the impression of almost unimaginable wealth, and the Emperor was reputed to be one of the richest men in the world. In fact, this was far from being the case. The annual income of the Imperial family as a whole, from all sources (Civil List, family lands, interest on bank deposits) amounted, it is true, to the impressive total of some £2½ million. But the Emperor's own share of it was limited to about £20,000, with another £20,000 going to his wife. The rest was distributed among the other sixty or so members of the family; the upkeep of the Imperial yacht, trains, stables, and palaces (of which there were seven); salaries and pensions to Court officials; presents (three times a year: Christmas, Easter, and the Emperor's nameday), wages, pensions and uniforms to servants (15,000 of them) and subsidies for the education of their children; subsidies to five theatres (including an Opera House), the Ballet, the Ballet School, the Academy of Arts and a great number of hospitals, orphanages, schools, homes for the blind and other institutions, which in other countries are usually financed out of public funds. At the time of his abdication, the Emperor's total personal fortune was estimated at a capital sum of £100,000 and his wife's at £150,000, but as numerous pensions had (or, rather, would have had) to be paid out of these sums, the remainder would have dwindled into insignificance.

(By comparison, the annual revenues of the much smaller British Royal family amounted at the time to just over £1½ million. Within that global sum, the King's Privy Purse amounted to £110,000, while another £64,000 was paid to him out of the revenues of the Duchy of Lancaster – £174,000 in all, compared to Nicholas's and Alexandra's joint £40,000. Added to this was the undisclosed income yielded by the King's very considerable personal fortune. The upkeep of the seven Royal palaces was partially financed out of other Departmental votes, as was the main expenditure in connection with the Royal yacht. No subsidies, of course, were paid out of this money to theatres, hospitals or charities.)

However, though the figures for the Civil List and the income from Imperial family lands were generally available, the public was apt hugely to exaggerate the Imperial family's wealth. Guests at receptions were dazzled by the proliferation of jewels, the gold-braided uniforms of soldiers and civilians, the vast array of servants in magnificent liveries, which gave every reception or festivity the appearance of a fairy-tale. In the evening the State apartments of the Catherine Palace in Tsarskoye Selo were resplendent with great crystal chandeliers lighting the enormous rooms with their polished parquet floors, their Persian rugs, their furniture of marble, mahogany, and rosewood, upholstered with velvet, silk, and satin. The air was fragrant with the smell of wood burning in huge porcelain stoves, mingling with incense carried about from room to room by footmen with powdered hair, in black, green, and scarlet liveries, and with flowers in tall Chinese vases, in lacquered pots, and silver bowls, taken from the palace's own greenhouses or brought by train from far-away Crimea. Curtains of sapphire and silver brocade shut out the world outside.

The Winter Palace, in which the Imperial family no longer lived and which, except for the Dowager Empress, it cordially disliked, came to life again at the beginning of every year for a short time. The New Year opened with a reception for the Diplomatic Corps. Then, at Epiphany, five days later, took place the ceremony of the Blessing of the Waters in commemoration of the Baptism of Christ. An ornate temporary pavilion was set up on the edge of the Neva by the Winter Palace, and a hole, referred to as the 'Jordan' for the occasion, was made in the ice of the river. The Emperor, surrounded by the highest dignitaries of Church and State, watched the Metropolitan immerse a cross in the 'Jordan' and took a small sip of the water thus consecrated, while guns boomed in salute from the Fortress of St Peter and St Paul across the river. The sight proved too much for the Tsar's former tutor, Charles Heath, a stout Protestant with English ideas of hygiene, and on at least one occasion he tried to remonstrate. The water, he said, may have been blessed, but it was none the less polluted. However, no notice was taken of his well-grounded scientific arguments, and no harm seems ever to have ensued from this ritual drinking.

But polluted water was not the only danger. In 1905, the year of the first revolution, the 'Jordan' ceremony was utilized in an attempt to assassinate the Emperor. The saluting guns were loaded with live ammunition instead of blank. But the marksmanship was evidently poor, for even at that close range and with the guns firing three times, there was only one casualty: a policeman standing behind the Emperor was seriously wounded. Of the other two shots, one broke a window in the Winter Palace and the other managed to miss not only the group in the pavilion, but even the vast hulk of the Winter Palace itself. It hit the nearby Admiralty building instead.

During 'the Season' which followed soon after, two or three great balls were given in the Winter Palace to which two to three thousand people were invited, and the Palace was all ablaze with colour and light. Inside, along the staircases and at every door, were posted troopers of the Cavalier Guards, gleaming with silver and gold and white, and Cossack Life Guards in red and blue uniforms. Palm trees and exotic Crimean plants, flowers of all kinds from the greenhouses of Tsarskoye Selo belied the weather outside – the bitter January night of St Petersburg. These magnificent pageants pleased the guests more than their hosts, it seems, and Nicholas and Alexandra hurried away as early in the evening as they decently could.

The grandest and most exclusive of such pageants took place in the evening of 22 January 1903, when 'the Season' was opened with a fancy-dress ball given in the Winter Palace. The period chosen was the seventeenth century. The Emperor wore the exact replica of Tsar Alexis's Court robes, and the Empress was dressed as his Consort, Tsaritsa Maria, in gold brocade covered with emeralds, pearls, and diamonds. The guests were all attired as boyars and boyarinyas of the time, with a profusion of jewels and furs. Old Russian dances were rehearsed for weeks in advance and danced by these living embodiments of a remote past. Later, that famous ball assumed an almost symbolic significance. For it proved to be the last of those great receptions which epitomized the social life of Imperial and aristocratic Russia. The Russo-Japanese war, followed by Russia's defeat, the revolution of 1905, the constitutional crisis, strikes, agrarian revolts, political assassinations and Government reprisals, the mounting tension, and, finally, the outbreak of World War I rendered festive Court life entirely inappropriate.

But just before the curtain came down for the last time, the fortuity of dates allowed the Dynasty to take, all unwittingly, its last formal bow on the stage of Russian history. In 1613, Michael, the first Romanov Tsar, was elected to the throne of Russia and duly crowned in Moscow. The year 1913 – the last before the cataclysm of war and revolution engulfed the old order – thus marked the 300th anniversary of Romanov rule. Official festivities, ceremonies and receptions took place all over Russia, and the last Romanov Tsar undertook a pilgrimage, retracing the steps of the first, from Michael's birth-place to Kostroma, where the crown had been offered to him, and finally to Moscow, to pray in the Cathedral of the Assumption, where both Michael and Nicholas had been anointed sovereigns of their country. As the Emperor and Empress travelled from one town to another and down the river Volga, thousands of their subjects, who had never seen them before, thronged to greet them. The greeting, it so turned out, was also a farewell.

It was a farewell to the Emperor, to the Dynasty, to the whole institution of Monarchy in Russia. And strangely, the Dynasty, in the person of its main representatives, did not seem to mind. Four years later, when, after Nicholas's abdication, the choice of Monarchy or Republic was placed in the hands of a future Constituent Assembly, the Emperor's cousin, grand-duke Nicholas Mikhailovich, declared that, if elected to the Assembly, he would vote for a Republic. The Emperor's brother, Michael, found himself more directly involved. The Crown, on the morrow of the Emperor's abdication, was offered to him (somewhat gingerly, without, it must be admitted, much enthusiasm). He refused to accept it without the sanction of the Constituent Assembly, but even before the Assembly had been convened, Kerensky's government anticipated its decision by proclaiming a Republic. It was, to Michael at least, an unexpected turn of events, but it left him entirely indifferent. That evening, 2 September 1917, he noted in his Diary: 'We woke up this morning to hear Russia proclaimed a Democratic Republic. What does it matter what the form of government will be, provided there is order and justice in the land.'

Since the Dynasty itself – including the member of it most directly involved (the grand-duke Michael) – viewed its own and the Monarchy's disappearance with perfect equanimity, almost with satisfaction (grand-duke Nicholas Mikhailovich), the lack of support for it among the population is not really surprising. Even the army made no move to save it. The officer corps had, in fact, become by that time largely apolitical. It was loyal, certainly, but its loyalty was, by and large, to the country as a whole rather than to the Emperor personally. The Guards were probably an exception in that they felt they had a special link with the Monarchy, a 'special relationship' to it. This was particularly true of those regiments which had members of the Imperial family serving in them, and many officers whom the Emperor knew socially. But the Emperor himself, after his abdication, tried to encourage the transfer of loyalty from his own person to the new regime, by calling on the troops in his last Order of the Day to stand by the Provisional Government and continue the war. The Provisional Government, it is

Countess Brassova, (extreme right), wife of the Emperor's younger brother Michael,
entertains friends to a summer al-fresco meal on the terrace of their country estate.
The little girl is her daughter Tata by her first marriage,
the dogs her mongrel Jack and the Grand Duke's poodle Cuckoo.

true, unwilling, presumably, to let the Emperor appear in a favourable light, suspended, for the occasion, its newly-granted freedom of the press and forbade newspapers to publish the Order. But its contents reached the Army staffs and no doubt facilitated the acceptance of the new regime by those who still had qualms about it on grounds of loyalty.

In a peasant country like Russia the army was, of course, an overwhelmingly peasant army. With the spread of education and the rise in educational standards, the same was inevitably becoming true of its officers, though the proportion of officers from the urban middle class was also rising, at the expense of those from gentry families. On the eve of Nicholas II's reign, officers of peasant origin made up only 5 per cent of the officer corps; by 1914 the figure rose to 19 per cent. By 1916 the immense casualties of the war helped to reinforce the normal social process, and in that year as much as 70 per cent of officer trainees were of peasant origin.* General Denikin, head of the White Army fighting against the Bolshevik forces, was no exception in being, like Lenin, the grandson of a serf: the same was true of many of his fellow-officers in the Russian Imperial General Staff.

Besides, technological advance increased the demand for technically qualified officers, irrespective of their social origin. This reinforced the steady rise in the number of officers from the urban middle class. By 1916 they supplied 26 per cent of officer trainees, while gentry families supplied a mere 4 per cent. The Guards, of course, formed an exception to this trend. They alone carried on the tradition, established very soon after their regiments were formed a couple of centuries before, of recruiting their officers exclusively from gentry families.

Paradoxically, at first sight, the officer corps remained 'noble'. The reason was that quite a low rank or even simply a decoration carried with it a patent of nobility – personal below the rank of colonel and hereditary for colonel and above.

* None of these figures includes Cossack officers, who were almost all of peasant origin, but were not so shown in statistics, since Cossacks were not officially registered as peasants. They were land cultivators in uniform, a distinction to which all Cossack males were entitled.

It is in any case difficult to talk about 'gentry' or 'nobility' in Russia for the Russians have no word for either. The usual term is *dvoryanstvo*, which covers both – and much more besides – without any real correspondence in meaning. For, like the peasants, the 'nobles' (*dvoryanye*) formed not a class, but an 'Estate'. Within it there were, in effect, several classes, in the western sense, and membership of the 'Estate' could be acquired fairly easily. It was, as has just been said, automatic following promotion to a certain rank in the Armed Forces (Army colonel, Naval captain) or the Civil Service, or even following the grant of a military or civil decoration. A somewhat lower rank or decoration entitled the holder to 'personal' or life nobility, which became inheritable if two generations – father and son – happened to be granted it. The degree of social mobility that this implied was, of course, very high indeed. Thus, while Lenin's grandfather had been a serf, Lenin himself was born a 'noble', since his father – the serf's son – had acquired hereditary *dvoryanstvo* on his appointment as Chief School Inspector with an appropriate Civil Service rank and the order of St Vladimir.

Titles proliferated since every member of a titled family had the right to bear the title, and every male of the family had the right to transmit it to his legitimate posterity for ever. There was only one native Russian title: *knyaz*. It is invariably translated as 'prince', making it sound royal to English ears. However, it was applicable to all direct descendants, however distant, of any ruler, however petty, who had at any time, however remote, ruled over any part, however small, of the territory which eventually became the Russian Empire. In the eighteenth century the Russian government introduced two new titles direct from Germany: *graf* (Count) and baron, which, for lack of a Russian equivalent, were left untranslated. At the same time it adopted the Western principle of bestowing titles as a mark of favour or reward for services rendered, and this further increased the number of 'princes'. Some of these 'princes' were found in modest and even menial occupations, such, for instance, as Leo Tolstoy's family butler, Vasiliy Trubetskoy, a descendant of a Lithuanian dynasty (dispossessed many centuries ago), and hence with a perfect right to his title of 'prince'.

All in all, it is hardly surprising that Russian *dvoryanye* should have been counted literally by the million: there were some 1.8 million of them at the beginning of Nicholas II's reign and probably about two million at the end of it. The overwhelming majority — about two-thirds — were hereditary.

It is difficult in the circumstances to identify *dvoryanstvo* with aristocracy, as is sometimes done in discussions about Tsarist Russia. However, some families within the *dvoryanstvo* did correspond closely in social standing and esteem to the British and international concept of aristocracy. Titled or untitled (for the name alone counted), they prided themselves on their illustrious lineage, whether truly ancient or due to relatively recent Royal favour, and a few of them enjoyed great wealth and landed property. Riches by themselves, however, were no passport to the charmed circle, and in any case few indeed were those whose wealth could be compared to their Western counterparts. A great fortune dating back to beyond the middle of the eighteenth century was quite exceptional. A Proustian analyst would note that in the world of Russian snobbery a Sheremetev (with or without the title of Count) would rank higher than many a (perhaps any) princely family, and that the poorer and untitled branch of the Sheremetevs outranked its titled millionaire cousins if only through its close blood relationship to the Emperor himself.

The country houses of even the most aristocratic and richest of these families were, by British standards, of very recent date — mostly nineteenth century and none earlier than mid-eighteenth — and (with very few exceptions) of relatively modest appearance. No medieval castles, no equivalent of the great Tudor mansions of the English countryside. The absence of a feudal system in the past, no law of entail, and the scarcity of building materials other than timber had seen to that. There were, of course, exceptional houses on a par (or almost) with Blickling or Chatsworth in England, though of later date. Such was Arkhangelskoye, an enormous nineteenth-century mansion belonging to the Yusupovs — now the home of retired Marshals of the Soviet Union — or Ostankino (now a museum), built a little earlier for the Sheremetevs. They were conceived on a palatial scale and housed precious collections of furniture, pictures, and objets d'art as well as a private theatre. More modest examples of architectural splendour were dotted about the countryside, particularly around Moscow, many built or influenced by Italian architects. By the end of the nineteenth century, the Crimea, with its near-Mediterranean climate, its sea, mountains, and magnificent scenery began to attract those in search of more exotic glamour. And there again, the Yusupovs, being the richest of Russian aristocrats, outshone all their peers and rivalled the Imperial family itself.

But on the whole, the Russian aristocracy were mainly absentee landowners who lived mostly in one of the two capitals, Moscow or St Petersburg, preferably the latter, where they occupied some function at Court or served in one of the smarter Guards regiments such as the Horse Guards or the Cavalier Guards (corresponding to the Household Cavalry in England), or received a Government appointment, which, however, was rarely that of a Minister of the Crown. Their influence could not be compared to that of the Peerage in England since they had no hereditary right to membership of a legislature, and whatever influence they did possess was exercised by them as individuals rather than as a group.

There was, of course, no hard and fast line of social demarcation between the topmost layers of the nobility and the old, but less illustrious or less fashionable and, on the whole, poorer *dvoryanstvo*, the true gentry in the British sense, who were more frequently found living on their estates and were active landowners if they were not civil servants, writers, musicians or professional men. The transition was gradual from the glittering aristocracy of St Petersburg, through what Tolstoy called the 'middle-upper class' (in which he included himself) to the middle gentry, with many ties of blood, and marriage, school, regiment, interests, friendship, and manners between them.

The popular picture of a vastly rich Russian aristocracy squandering its millions in sumptuous living of oriental splendour has little foundation in fact, if only because the millions were not there to spend. Great private fortunes on a scale typical of industrial societies whether European or American were beyond the reach of such a predominantly agricultural country as Russia. It is doubtful if even the richest half-dozen aristocratic families of Russia, including the Imperial family, could compete with the Rockefellers or the Astors or the Vanderbilts or the Rothschilds, and few if any of them could boast of fortunes comparable to those of their social peers in the United Kingdom, such, for instance, as the Ducal families of Sutherland or Bedford or Devonshire. Ostentatious living or 'conspicuous consumption' certainly existed, and there are many stories of extravagant behaviour by Russia's *jeunesse dorée*, but these could easily be matched or even outshone by similar stories told about the *jeunesse dorée* of any other country. Kshesinskaya's description of the last dinner party she gave a few days before the Revolution engulfed her and her world is sometimes quoted as an example of such extravagance. Yet 'the top ten' in Britain or America or '*les 200 familles*' in France would hardly have been as impressed by it as the famous dancer, touchingly oblivious of its vulgarity, was herself. Mistress at different times of several members of the Imperial family (including, before his marriage, the Emperor himself) and finally the wife of one of them, she enjoyed considerable wealth by Russian standards, or, at least, had easy access to it, and the party in her estimation and that of her friends was a dazzling affair. She gave it, she says, 'for twenty-four friends, for which I brought out my finest Limoges service, my Danish service for the fish, and gilt cutlery copied from two sets belonging to Catherine the Great which could be seen at the Hermitage. This had been given to me by [Grand-Duke] André. The guests were dazzled by the dinner table decorated with forget-me-nots and real lace. It was my swan song in Petrograd, my last dinner party before the Revolution. I brought out countless precious trinkets and works of art which had been stored since the beginning of the war (among other things there was a superb collection of artificial flowers made of precious stones and a small gold fir tree, with branches shimmering with little diamonds). There were so many of these things that I complained to my sister I had not enough room to display them. The fates were to take a cruel vengeance for these words: a few days later there was nothing left to display.'

The last phrase reads like an epitaph, a Society hostess's despairing *sic transit gloria mundi*.

The fact is that the Russians' behaviour and entertainments struck foreign observers as extravagant and costly not because they really were more so than in the West, but because they were different — to conform to Russian tastes and customs. Russians like jewellery, are fond of good food, and are very hospitable. And so foreigners often remarked on the impressive show of jewels Russians liked to display, on the gargantuan meals with innumerable courses and the constant stream of guests at all meals and all times of the day, often turning up unexpectedly and unannounced for lunch, tea or dinner, and on the hordes of servants whose numbers seemed to exceed any real need for them, and who treated their masters as their masters treated them — with a familiarity, a *sans gêne* which foreigners often found embarrassing.

In the country, the enormous distances and bad roads imposed a hospitality very different from what was usual in Western Europe. Guests came to stay for days, sometimes for weeks, and when they did were entertained as lavishly as the host could afford. A favourite pastime was shooting and hunting. Not fox-hunting as practised in England. Russians thought it too formal and artificial and preferred bigger game such as bear or elk or wolves when these were natural to the region. The wolf hunt was probably the most exciting, but it was becoming an increasingly rare entertainment. Tolstoy in his *War and Peace* describes one of these wolf hunts in which the hounds attack the beast from both sides, aiming to seize him by the throat. At a suitable, if risky, moment a huntsman jumps from his horse down on to the wolf's back and stabs him in the heart. However, such a virile method of despatching wolves was followed only in the summer and anyway demanded more initiative than most men possessed. A more usual way was to shoot them in the winter, with beaters driving them towards the guns, who stood motionless, dressed in white. The same method was adopted for other game and constituted one of the great sports of those who had an estate to live in or to go to.

In fact, the majority of the rich and middle *dvoryanye*, even those who depended for their livelihood on employment in the city, had a family estate to which they went if only on an occasional visit, though some, of course, stayed on their estates all the year round, tied to them by farming or by participation in the local administration. These family estates – 'gentry nests', Turgenev called them – are familiar to all readers of Russian literature. A British observer who spent some years in Russia on the eve of the first World War, thought them a characteristic feature of the Russian landscape and described them just before they finally disappeared in the cataclysm of war and revolution.

'The house', he writes, 'stands preferably on a river bank or on a hill-side. It is half-hidden amidst a grove of trees. Frequently, especially if the house was built, as a great many of the houses of the country gentry were, at the beginning of the nineteenth century, it has a veranda and a balcony supported by massive white columns. Near the house there is almost sure to be a lime-tree avenue, leading to an orchard of apple, pear and cherry trees. A flower garden, sometimes with artificial ponds, and a variety of outbuildings complete the number of immediate appurtenances of the manor-house. Indoors a wide entrance-hall, a big dining room, a drawing room, a kitchen full of busy chattering life, stairs leading to all sorts of quaint nooks and corners, well-stocked store-rooms, libraries often containing old and valuable books, pretty, old-fashioned mahogany furniture, family portraits on the walls and generally a snug and soothing sense of leisure, security, and remoteness from the bustle of the world. Such is the home of the average *pomiesh-chik*' – a landowner or country squire.

It was this social group – 'the average *pomieshchik*' – that more than any other in Russia contributed to the cultural life of the country and earned for the last century of Imperial rule the name of 'gentry civilization', *dvoryanskaya kultura*. Pushkin, the Aksakovs, Tolstoy, Turgenev, Glinka, Tchaikovsky, Diaghilev all came from it. So did Dostoyevsky, though he marks the transition to that other group which constituted the vast bulk of the Russian 'nobility' – country or urban. The town 'nobles' of this lower social level corresponded in income, occupation, and social standing to anything from a petty to a middle bourgeoisie in France and England. From their ranks came many local government officials, middle-grade civil servants, army officers, doctors (such as Dostoyevsky's father). Often they had a stake in the country – a family farm where they went on leave or whenever freedom from their regular employment allowed them. (Dostoyevsky's father went to his once too often: his peasants – it was in the time of serfdom – murdered him in revenge for his brutalities.)

Within this group of *dvoryanstvo*, most of those who derived all their income from land could be compared to medium and small farmers in England, but numerous were those whose acres were no more extensive – and were sometimes less extensive – than the fields of the peasants around them. In such cases there was nothing but their nominal *dvoryanstvo* to distinguish them from other villagers. They ploughed and sowed and harvested alongside the peasants, lived in similar houses or huts and shared the peasants' interests.

One group of these peasant 'nobles' had a curious origin. It was formed of Tartars invited by the Lithuanian government in the early Middle Ages as a military force to defend the country from invasion by Teutonic knights. They were allowed to keep their Muslim faith and to build mosques, were given land to cultivate and granted titles and the status of nobility. Their descendants in the beginning of the twentieth century preserved all these privileges – a tiny enclave of Islam on the shores of the Baltic Sea. Most of these 'nobles' had small farms, but they supplemented their income by working mainly as tanners or as restaurant waiters in large towns.

Yet officially the *dvoryanstvo* was referred to as the 'privileged Estate'. By the twentieth century reasons for this were historic rather than actual. At the time of serfdom the *dvoryanye* alone had the right to own serfs, they were free from certain taxes, they were not subject to recruitment though they were expected to serve in the armed forces if they did not choose the civil service instead. But the reforms of Alexander II in the nineteenth century gradually eroded these privi-leges. Serfdom was abolished, the tax laws were changed, universal military service was intro-duced. In local government, it is true, the *dvoryanstvo* still enjoyed prerogatives denied to other 'Estates': so-called Land Captains – all of them *dvoryanye* – supervised peasant self-governing institutions, Marshals of the Gentry exercised important local government functions.

Court functionaries and the officers of at least the smarter Guards regiments were in fact, though not by law, all *dvoryanye*, and within the *dvoryanstvo* itself certain schools (the Imperial Corps of Pages, the Alexander Lyceum and the Imperial Law School for boys, the Smolny Institute for girls) were reserved for the children of the higher grades of nobility.

But the tide was inexorably turning against the *dvoryanye*, and Chekhov's *Cherry Orchard* was being re-enacted in real life all over the country. Land — their main economic basis — was slipping away from them and into the hands partly of speculators, but overwhelmingly of peasants, who, by the closing years of the Tsarist regime owned or leased about 90 per cent of the sown area of the country. Besides, the age of industry had come and with it the rise of the capitalist *entrepreneur* who was taking the place of the country squire as the chief power in the land. This process, it is true, was halted by the Revolution, but when it was, the issue was decided in favour of neither. The peasants, it may be added, were allowed to keep their land about a decade longer — until deprived of it by agricultural collectivization.

But if the *entrepreneur*, the speculator was not to be classed with either 'Nobles' or 'Peasants', who then was he? What class did he belong to? In West European terms he would have been included in the 'Middle Classes' (whether 'upper' or 'lower' or in between), the *bourgeoisie* (*grande* or *petite*). In Russia, where social divisions went not by class, but by 'Estate', he would have belonged, typically, to an 'Estate' of his own, which happened to be the most numerous after the peasants: the '*Mestchánstvo*' (13 million strong at the beginning of the reign and getting on for twenty at the end of it). And he would have been referred to as a *mestchanín* (plural: *mestchánye*).

It is a difficult term to translate. In every-day parlance it was used synonymously with the French *bourgeois*, with all the French connotations of that word. Literally, *mestchanín* means a townsman, a burgher — a reference to a remote past when this is exactly what he was, and this is also, of course, the literal sense of the French word *bourgeois*. It is also true that within the *mestchánstvo* as an 'Estate', was included the same category of person as is usually covered by the terms *bourgeoisie* and 'middle class': traders,

bankers and businessmen, army officers and the *intelligentsia*, doctors, lawyers, school teachers, university dons and other professional men, shop keepers and shop assistants, and office workers. There was, of course, no reason at all why a member of the 'Nobility' should not have become one of these, and many of them did. But it is probably true that most people employed in these occupations were, in fact, *mestchánye*.

However, the Russian concept of *mestchánstvo* as an officially recognized social group was both narrower and wider than the *bourgeoisie*, the middle class. It was narrower because it excluded industrialists, merchants, traders and business-men who had joined a 'Merchant Guild' and thereby become 'Merchants', i.e. members of the Merchant Estate. It also excluded the clergy, who formed a special category, and men in the armed forces and the civil service who had reached a certain rank or obtained a decoration. These, as has already been said, became 'Nobles'.

On the other hand, those who had left their villages to work in town or in a factory or mine, and had officially cut their links with their village commune, were, all of them, registered as *mestchánye* — in other words, the city proletariat, the industrial workers, the working-class popula-tion generally. Besides, also registered as *mest-chánye*, were all illegitimate children and children from foundling hospitals. They continued to be such, irrespective of occupation, unless, later on in life, they successfully applied for a change of status or transferred themselves through their personal achievements into another 'Estate', such as the 'Nobility' or the 'Merchants'. But there was one non-middle-class element within the *mestchánstvo* which, numerically, was more important than any other, since it comprised about half the total 'Estate'. It consisted of men and women who lived and worked on the land and were indistinguish-able from peasants or agricultural labourers, except that for some — generally, historic — reason they had been registered in the past not as 'peasants', but as '*mestchánye*'.

Thus came about the curious fact that in Imperial Russia a man need not have been a peasant to be a peasant. He could be a factory operative, a miner, a cabby or some other city dweller, and yet, in the eyes of the law, be a peasant just the same. For in the eyes of the law social status was conferred not by a person's occupation, but by the official 'Estate' (in the medieval sense) within which he (or she) was registered and which was duly marked in his (or her) passport: 'Noble', 'Merchant', 'Burgher', 'Peasant', 'Cleric' (which included all priests and deacons and their families, monks etc.). To join some of the 'Estates' was relatively easy; it was certainly easier to become a 'Noble' than to become a 'Peasant'. For the former, a decoration or the achievement of a modest rank in the armed forces or the civil service sufficed. The procedure to join the latter would have been so complicated, not to say bizarre, that it was next to impossible to become a 'peasant' unless born into that social group. Nor was it easy to cease being one. 'Peasants' who had long abandoned all connection with agriculture and were employed in factories, mines, urban occupations of all sorts either seasonally or permanently, remained registered as 'peasants' unless their commune released them from membership and they were thus able to join another 'Estate' – that of *mestchánye* (Burghers), for example, or 'Merchants'. But this was not easy for reasons which were financial and economic as well as social and traditional. For though they made up about four-fifths of the total population of the Empire (and in some provinces almost the totality of it), peasants were subject to laws and regulations which set them sharply apart from the remaining fifth. They had their own courts and their own judges elected by village councils and empowered to deal with civil cases on the basis of 'customary' law rather than the law of the State generally applicable to other social groups.

Until the first years of this century, when Stolypin's reforms set out to revolutionize the entire structure of peasant life, all peasants in Great Russia, though not in other parts of the Empire, were registered as members of communes each of which owned the land the peasant cultivated, and was responsible for the payment by its members of all financial dues to the Government. It followed, therefore that any peasant who found employment outside his commune – as an industrial or mine worker, as cab driver in town or as casual labourer in some seasonal occupation far away from home – was still tied to it by his financial obligations on the one hand and by the land allotted to him on the other. For the commune was obliged to allot land to all its members irrespective of whether they were present or absent, or whether they cultivated it themselves or with hired labour or let their family cultivate it or lease it to other peasants. Besides, apart from his right to a piece of land, a peasant never lost his right to participate in the commune's deliberations and decisions if he chose to appear in person at the meeting of the village council. These mutual rights and obligations ceased only with the commune's formal consent, usually obtained with great difficulty. The peasant would then have to leave his commune and either become a member of another or opt out of his peasant status altogether and be registered as, say, 'Burgher' or 'Merchant'. But while he was officially recognized as a peasant he was, together with all the other men of his village, entitled to decide on every aspect of life in his commune – from the choice of a shepherd to the distribution and redistribution of the fields or the purchase of additional land.

The aspect of a Russian village varied enormously even within the borders of Great Russia alone, as distinct from Ukraine or the Caucasus or the Baltic provinces or any other part of the Empire. As a rule, the houses (*izbá*), each with its own vegetable plot, stretched out on either side of a very broad street or, rather, unmade-up road, all but impassable in spring and autumn when rain and melting snow turned its surface into slushy mud.

Since timber was plentiful, houses were usually built of wood – log cabins one or two storeys high, with sharply sloping thatched or shingle roofs. A poor peasant would have no more than one living-room with, generally, though not always, an entrance lobby, a store-room (*klet*) at the side and another store-room (*podklét*) below. However, since the living-room was rarely built at soil level, but several feet above it, the *podklét* could not, strictly speaking, qualify as a cellar.

Whatever furniture there was stood in the living-room – a large table, a bench going round the walls, shelves with pots and pans on them, sometimes a cupboard where wooden spoons and eating bowls were kept, a samovar, two or three chairs perhaps, a vat or tub with water for washing, and – most important of all – a stove about

Setting out for the fields in birch-bark boots and leggings, 1882. This is at Simbirsk (now Ulyanovsk) on the Volga where I. N. Ulyanov was Chief Public Schools Inspector and where his son Vladimir (Lenin) was born in 1870.

five feet long and four feet wide, made of brick or clay, with a flat top high above the floor. It was a multi-purpose affair, used for heating, baking bread, cooking, and — especially by the children and the elderly — for sleeping on. A bed was rare. Those with no place on the stove, slept on straw on the floor or on the benches or on boards slung between two posts (*poláti*).

In a corner of the living-room — referred to as the 'Red' (or, rather the Beautiful, since this was the word's original meaning) corner — at least one icon hung on the wall, and every man would, on entering, doff his cap, make the sign of the cross and bow in the direction of that corner before speaking to his family or his host.

None of the other rooms — neither the entrance lobby nor the two store-rooms — was heated. In the lower store-room (*podklét*) chickens and sometimes calves or lambs were often kept, and in the summer some members of the family slept in the upper store-room (*klet*). In many parts of Russia it was customary to make up a bed for a newly-married couple for their wedding night in one of the two store-rooms.

Directly adjoining the house, but not on the side of the village road, was a yard with a shed for livestock and another for agricultural instruments and equipment, carts, sledges and so on, and sometimes a grain store.

Every Saturday the whole village would repair to the communal bath-house — similar to a Finnish *sauna* — with a large brick stove on which water was thrown to produce steam. The bathers lay on shelves against the wall — the higher the hotter — and beat themselves and each other with birch twigs for greater effect.

The following day, Sunday, being the day of rest (except at harvest time), started with Mass in church, a timber building, like the houses surrounding it, with a belfry surmounted by an onion-shaped dome, often painted blue or green. Mass, which it would have been unthinkable to avoid, lasted a fairly long time, sometimes as much as a couple of hours, during which the congregation either stood or knelt. The midday meal on that day was, for those who could afford it, rather better than it was on the other days of the week. The relatively well-off would even have meat, a welcome addition to the usual diet of rye bread, buckwheat porridge, cabbage, and salted cucumber washed down with tea or *kvas*, a kind of weak ale made from fermented rye bread. Older men would gather in the village inn, where they would gossip and drink innumerable cups of tea; vodka, too, but mostly it was left for festivals and great occasions, such as marriages and christenings.

The young would play games — *gorodkí* (something like skittles)·or *laptá*, a form of rounders, a great favourite, this — or there would be dancing to the accompaniment of an accordion. The best clothes would be donned, home-made and traditional still in most parts of the country, but gradually being ousted by articles of wholesale manufacture. The women might exchange their inevitable head-kerchief for a *kokóshnik*, a tall headdress decorated with pearls and gold ornaments according to the means of the wearer, and put on a sleeveless slip known as a *sarafán*. Men might sport a coloured shirt — red was the favourite colour — top boots, if they could afford them, and baggy trousers of a kind inherited from the Tartars centuries ago and still known by their Tartar name, slightly corrupted: *sharováry*.

On ordinary days the clothes were, of course, more utilitarian and drab. Men wore a shirt loose over their trousers, with a belt round the waist. Hence the point of Bismarck's jibe that a Russian's trustworthiness could be judged by the way he wore his shirt. We should, he said, beware of those who tucked their shirts into their trousers (i.e. the Europeanized urban minority). If a peasant wore anything over his shirt, it was a fairly long coat — a caftan — and, if the weather was cold, a sheepskin overcoat on top of that, which he used as a blanket at night. A fur-cap, preferably with ear-flaps, was essential in winter; in the summer the usual headgear was a peaked cap, though high hats made of felt were still occasionally seen. However, though often described and seen in many photographs and illustrations, the tall hats had, by the twentieth century, begun their trek to ethnographical museums. In the summer, too, poor peasants (men and women) went about either barefoot or in bast shoes (*lápti*), with a kind of puttees (*onúchi*) wrapped round the legs. In the winter the universal footwear was *válenki* (felt boots usually high enough to cover the calf of the leg), somewhat ungainly and shapeless, yet effective for keeping the feet warm.

It should again be stressed, however, that all the above descriptions and remarks apply exclusively to Great Russia. In areas outside Great Russia — in the Ukraine, Poland, the Baltic provinces etc. — customs, dress, houses, villages were entirely different. In Ukraine, peasant houses (*kháta*), grouped together rather than strung out along the road, were built mostly of clay and wattle, white-washed and with thatched roofs. They were, on the whole roomier and better kept, and peasants had a higher standard of living. In the Baltic provinces villages closely resembled those in Scandinavia or North Germany. In the Caucasus they could be compared to Syrian or Lebanese villages, with small stone huts (*sáklya*) clinging on to the mountain side. In Central Asia villages and village life were not very different from what they were in Iran or Afghanistan.

The distinguishing feature of Great Russia, responsible for much in the character of the population, its customs, and its standard of living, was its system of peasant property. Pastures, meadows, and forests were all held in common, but the fields were parcelled out among households. To achieve maximum equality and avoid the possibility of some peasants getting a disproportionate quantity of bad or of good land, the fields were divided into strips, each separated by a narrow grass balk — twenty or thirty strips to one household sometimes — lying at a considerable distance from each other. Moreover, the land was periodically redistributed by the decision of the commune to suit the changing number and composition of households. The results, of course, were disastrous for agricultural production and for any kind of individual initiative, since practically all improvement and experimentation was checked by the dependence of the strips on each other and no one was willing to spend time, labour and capital on the long-term improvement of land which could, after the next redistribution, be allotted to someone else. It cannot even be said that the effort expended on avoiding extremes of wealth and poverty among peasants had any conspicuous success. Luck or accidents — a fire, sickness, loss of livestock — personal defects and qualities led to the impoverishment of some and the enrichment of others. A poor peasant might cede the whole or part of his plot or plots to his more successful neighbour and drift into towns to try his luck as a factory hand. Or he might become an agricultural labourer, work locally, and occasionally, if he came from North or Central European Russia, trudge south to help gather in the harvest and cut the hay and then trudge back again in time for the harvest in his own province. A successful peasant might buy land from a neighbouring landowner or from the Peasant Bank, and this would not be subject to distribution among the other members of the commune. He might become the local tradesman and sell his goods on credit, or become the village usurer and if his interest rates were high and his terms stiff he would be known as a *kulák* (literally, a fist), a term afterwards applied by Stalin for propaganda purposes to all peasants, whatever their economic standing, unwilling to join a Collective or a State Farm, or in any way objectionable to the local Party or Government authorities or bosses.

The spread of the cooperative movement, with more and more cooperative shops opening in villages in the 1900s was, however, undermining the private trader's position in villages by providing goods and services at considerably lower prices. It also helped to promote the use of modern agricultural machinery, though the primitive wooden plough continued to be all too much in evidence, particularly in the more remote provinces.

Under the impact of reforms introduced by the Prime Minister Stolypin after the 1905 revolution, conditions of peasant life were beginning to change rapidly. To improve agricultural methods and stimulate private enterprise the Government set out to break the commune and increase peasant holdings. The peasants were encouraged to leave the commune, claim their share of the land as their private property and consolidate their scattered strips into small-holdings or farms, as was already the case in most other parts of the Empire outside Great Russia. At the same time the acquisition of more land by the peasants was facilitated by financial assistance for settlement beyond the Urals and by grants-in-aid and relatively low-interest credits for the purchase of land belonging to the State, the Imperial family, and the gentry. The peasants readily availed themselves of the opportunity to extend their property and by 1916 all but about 11 per cent of the total sown area of the country was owned (or, more rarely, leased) by them. (Their share of total land was much smaller, but that was because State, Crown, and landowners' property was to a large extent either covered by forests or unsuitable for cultivation). At the same time the peasants' share of the total livestock was even greater than that of the sown area: by 1916 it reached about 94 per cent.

About a quarter of peasant households cultivating communal land were by then able to consolidate their holdings. Some of them set up new houses on the farms thus created, away from the villages they had been living in, but most of them found this type of arrangement uncongenial and unfriendly and preferred to stay in their old homes. However, the reform did not have the time to be fully implemented. Lenin was bitterly opposed to it. He thought its success would jeopardize the chances of a revolution, and when the revolution did take place it swept away the reform and abolished all private ownership of land either by peasants or by anyone else.

A considerable number of peasants supplemented their income by working at some form of cottage industry in which the whole family took part. Usually it was a leisure occupation only, during the many months of enforced idleness in the winter months, but sometimes it represented the family's chief and even – though this was rare – its only source of income, involving the entire family the whole year round. Everyone took part in it, from grandparents however old, to grandchildren however young, provided they were physically (and mentally) capable of doing the work. Since timber was the most readily available raw material, objects made of wood were the commonest of all cottage industry products – from spoons to furniture. Jute and flax were frequently used (ropes, articles of clothing), and there were specialists in metals – from pins to samovars – clay (mostly pottery), leather (shoes, belts), and so on. Specialization was regional: samovars in the Tula Province, gloves in Nizhni-Novgorod (now Gorki) and so forth. Some villages specialized exclusively in icons. The products of one such village (Palekh) have become familiar in the West since the

Revolution, when the artisans were made to switch over from icons to illustrations of folk and fairy tales, painted, by using a special process, on boxes made of papier-mâché treated to look and even feel like wood.

Sometimes the raw material was supplied from outside – cotton, for instance – and the artisans (known as *kustari*) would then work for a fixed market. In that case the distinction between peasant and industrial worker tended to become blurred. It was, in any case, difficult to estimate the total number of *kustari*, since it was uncertain who should be included in that category. Estimates varied from $1\frac{1}{2}$ million to 15 million, which is, in effect, a confession of ignorance, but 2–4 million seems to be a reasonable range. At the same time the number of factory operatives was only about 1.6 million (at the end of the century). To say that the main point about the industrial proletariat in Tsarist Russia is that it did not exist is, therefore, tempting. But it is not accurate. At the beginning of Nicholas II's reign the number of men and women who could be classed as the industrial labour force, working not only in factories, but also in transport and mines, was estimated at about $2\frac{1}{2}$ million; at the end of it there were about twice as many. But since industrial development in that period was extremely rapid (coal output nearly quadrupled, steel more than tripled, cotton yarn doubled, oil nearly doubled), they usually belonged to only the first or second generation of industrial workers and had kept their links with the villages from which they had come; many of them still owned plots of land, were members of village communes and had their cousins and sometimes parents, brothers and sisters working as peasants. To many of them their villages remained 'home' – so much so that in the years immediately following the 1917 Revolution a great proportion of the industrial proletariat simply disappeared, melted away into the countryside.

But quite apart from the exceptional years of the Revolution, come summer and harvest time, thousands of industrial workers would normally leave the production line and the factory floor and troop back to their villages to help gather in the crops. Conversely, with the approach of winter, peasants in their tens of thousands, often accompanied by their wives and children, would

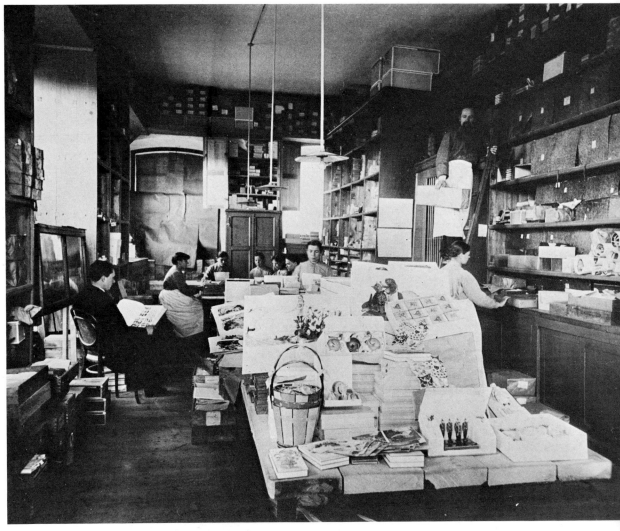

One of the workshops of Abrikosov and Sons, confectioners, 1888.

be streaming into towns and manufacturing centres in search of work. As a rule, they were organized in groups known as *artél*, with an elected leader, an 'elder' (*stárosta*), at the head of each. The 'elder' was paid a few kopeks (equivalent to a penny or two in present British currency) a week by each member of his *artél*, and in exchange would make himself responsible for finding work for it on arrival in town. If successful, he would draw up an agreement with the employer, sign it or, more usually, put his mark at the bottom of it, and hand over to him his passport and those of his mates, to be returned on expiry of contract.

These seasonal workmen were as a rule accommodated in barracks of varying quality, each large enough to house several hundred people. Kitchen and dining hall generally occupied the entire ground floor, while dormitories were distributed throughout the upper floors – one type for single men, another for married couples and a third for unmarried women with children. The 'rent', if such it could be called, amounted to the equivalent of 5 or 6 new pence per month and included heating, lighting and the use of the kitchen stove. Those who could afford to pay three or four times as much, say 15 to 25 new pence per month, were lodged not in dormitories, but in houses with large rooms capable of accommodating whole families. The rooms, it is true, were somewhat spartanly furnished: one large table, benches, bedsteads, and two or three cupboards. According to some sources, the rooms were warm and well ventilated as a rule, though many, of course, fell much below the average in this and other respects. Others paint a considerably more sombre picture of the conditions in which the average Russian industrial operative had to live and work.

Seasonal workers were almost always paid on a piece-work basis, the achievements of each being recorded in the factory books and also by the *artél* elder on short wooden sticks – a stick per worker – on which notches were made, whose significance was clear to the illiterate. The wages would then be paid to the elder, who was responsible for distributing the money among his group. This curious dependence on, and implicit trust in, the *artél*'s elected representative extended to the purchase of the *artél*'s daily food. It was bought by the elder for the *artél* as a whole, including the women and children, after he had collected the money for it. Not that he had to exercise much imagination in choosing it. Breakfast, such as it was, consisted of no more than rye bread and *kvas*, and the midday and evening meals inevitably of rye bread again and a thick cabbage soup. Occasionally hunks of meat were added to the soup and, perhaps, some sour-cream (*smetána*) of which Russians are particularly fond. Many, though by no means all, factory managements supplied tea and sugar free of charge. Any profit made by the elder in the course of the season was returned to the *artél* in equal shares, less a small percentage which the elder got for his pains and as an inducement to make as large a profit as possible.

If the factory or mill was situated outside town and employed a labour force above a certain minimum, the management was legally bound to provide free of charge a school for the children of the operatives as well as certain amenities such as a hospital, a library and a bath-house. This, of course, applied to permanent personnel as much as to seasonal workers. In any case, with the development of industry, the latter were gradually losing their significance relative to the permanent staff which accounted for the bulk of the labour force.

But the very rapidity of industrial development and therefore of the expansion of industrial employment brought with it the same stresses and abuses as in other countries at the same stage of industrialization – miserable living conditions, low wages, exploitation – but they brought them a generation later and concentrated them within a shorter space of time, making them less bearable and more dramatic. Moreover, men's consciences had by then become much more alive to the evils of social misery and injustice, and the revolutionary potential of dissatisfaction and unrest was more clearly realized and more efficiently organized than had been the case in other countries in the past. This was one of the penalties Russia had to pay for joining so late in the game of economic development.

It is difficult to speak of the living standards of industrial workers in Russia (meaning the Russian Empire) as a whole. They differed vastly over a vast territory and were, for instance, much less satisfactory in Moscow than in St Petersburg or Russian Poland. Russian factories were generally organized on a bigger scale than was usual in the West and employed a greater number of men and women. (This was partly due to the scarcity of managerial talent, which had to be spread over all existing industrial establishments.) It was difficult to supply adequate accommodation for such large concentrations of people, especially since most factories were situated outside towns. Some factory owners tried to solve the problem by building barracks, not only for seasonal workers as described above, but for their permanent staff as well, but though some succeeded in providing excellent accommodation, all too often workers were lodged in conditions of extreme squalor and overcrowding. Of course, there were exceptions in the other direction too. The enormous steel foundry and arms factory at Izhevsk, for example, provided each family with its own timber-built house standing in its own garden plot, but this, alas, was anything but typical.

Wages were low, though rising after 1905. Even so, by 1910 the average factory operative received less than half the average wage of a British workman at the time, though he lagged far less behind some continental countries, such as Belgium. Besides, in many cases, he, or at least his family if it remained behind in its village, could rely on an additional income in kind from the piece of land he possessed as member of a peasant commune. Unfortunately, the existence of an additional source of income was usually taken into account by the factory management and therefore tended to depress the level of wages paid. The increasing 'urbanization' of the factory worker and the breaking of village ties led to the rapid disappearance of this additional income and made a rise in wages more essential than ever.

Alongside the rise in wages there was a fall in hours of work. It was considered a great achievement when an $11\frac{1}{2}$-hour working day (and a shorter one for night workers, women, and adolescents) was forced on unwilling employers in 1897, yet only a few years later – in about 1905–6 – a nine- to ten-hour working day was introduced for most, and an eight-hour day for many, workers.

In 1903 an important Act was passed establishing the liability of employers for accidents in factories, free medical care, sickness benefit and pensions for those who had met with an accident at work and were unable to carry on working either temporarily or permanently. Trade unions with severely circumscribed powers were legalized in 1906, though their existence and activity preceded the law which allowed them by over a year. In 1912 new legislation extended and improved the 1903 Act, workers' compensation was considerably increased and disability payments raised, the scheme to be administered mainly by the workers themselves. The most recent Western analyst of the 1912 legislation finds in it 'numerous deficiencies', but is bound to admit that at least 'in its provisions for medical care [it] went well beyond that offered in any other country'.

Much of the Russian labour legislation was based on the German model, but it would have been more satisfactory if it had been more rigorously applied in practice. As it was, evasions of the law were frequent and conditions of life of factory operatives suffered in consequence.

Both the labour legislation and the rise of wages were due largely to trade union activity as well as (and mainly) to the strikes which occurred with increasing frequency from the last quarter of the nineteenth century. In theory, strikes were forbidden right up to 1907; in practice, however, they took place on an impressive scale, often involving well over half the total Russian industrial labour force in support of demands not only economic – such as wages, hours, and conditions of work – but also purely political. In fact, during the years of revolutionary and semi-revolutionary unrest, 1905–8, political strikes, intensified by the 'Bloody Sunday' tragedy, far exceeded those waged for economic reasons, which in some years made up hardly a third of the total number, but were on the whole surprisingly successful.

Often what started as a strike in pursuit of economic aims ended as a call for political action. The events which, at the time of the Russo-Japanese war, precipitated the revolution of 1905 had as their immediate background a strike for an eight-hour day and a higher minimum wage in the great Putilov metallurgical and arms factory in St Petersburg. Within a few days the strike spread to other factories as well. Led by a body known as the Assembly of Russian Factory and Mill Workers, at the head of which stood a politically minded priest, George Gapon, the strikers were organized into forming a mass demonstration to present a petition to the Tsar. On Sunday, 9 January 1905, a vast crowd of 200,000 people converged on the square in front of the Winter Palace. The demand for shorter hours and higher pay was by then forgotten. The petition called for an end to the war with Japan, a Constitution, the disestablishment of the Church, free and universal education, a graduated income tax in place of indirect taxation etc. That the Tsar was living in Tsarskoye Selo and not in the Winter Palace and could not, therefore, receive a deputation from the crowd, was not known by the rank and file of the demonstrators, though it is unlikely that their leaders were equally ignorant of the fact. But the aim of the demonstrators was to demonstrate, not to be received by

A hunting party. Hunting expeditions in remote parts of the country were sometimes accompanied by guides like the Terek or Kuban Cossack shown in the picture with his fowling-piece.

the Tsar. However, be that as it may, when, on the morning of that fateful Sunday the huge procession reached the Palace Square, it was stopped by the police and army troops and ordered to disperse. It failed to do so and the troops, after one blank volley, fired straight into the crowd, killing over a hundred people. It is difficult to exaggerate the effect and repercussions of that disastrous day. Riots and demonstrations flared up with increased vigour, the universities closed down in sign of protest, strikes spread throughout the country, acts of terrorism started again, the first victim that year being the Grand Duke Serge, Governor-General of Moscow. The revolution of 1905 – the dress rehearsal for 1917, as it was afterwards called – had begun.

Twelve years later history repeated itself: a war in which Russia was doing badly, a strike in the Putilov factory for higher wages and shorter hours, the spreading of strikes to other factories and industrial establishments, the increasing emphasis on political rather than economic demands. This time the Government did not have sufficient power − or sufficient backing in the country as a whole − to fight back effectively, and its freedom of action was in any case severely limited by the war to which it was committed. Precisely one week after the Putilov strike had begun the Emperor abdicated the throne.

In the summer of 1913, when the Emperor was still on his throne (fairly firmly, it was thought, in spite of all the tension), Russia was celebrating the Tercentary of its Imperial House. The festivities opened with a State visit to Moscow of the Emperor and his family. In the course of it the Emperor was to receive a deputation of the representatives of the various 'Estates' − the Nobility, the Merchants, the Peasants, the Burghers. The ceremonial was drawn up in accordance with an immutable protocol: the Nobility to be received first in the principal room of the Kremlin Palace, the Merchants to follow in the second. It was submitted to the Emperor and approved by him as a matter of course. Great, therefore, was the consternation of the Minister of the Court responsible for the arrangements when he was informed by the spokesman of the Merchants that they were refusing to attend. 'In Moscow,' they had instructed their spokesman to say, 'we are the hosts. It would be unseemly for us to meet the Emperor in the second room of the Palace.' Their plea was accepted, but not before it had been communicated to the Emperor himself and had received his consent. The Merchants (including the industrial magnates) and the Nobility (including Court officials) were duly placed in the same room − the first room, but in two separate groups, facing each other. Did anyone at the time note the symbolism of these two confronting social orders? Or of the last-minute change in protocol? The shift of power within the State? Probably. But what few could have guessed was that the shift had come too late: the world in which it mattered had only four more years to live.

However, at the time it mattered greatly. The 'Merchants', the men of business, were the manifestation (they would have said the cause) of Russia's economic development, the creators and owners of wealth which had long begun to slip away from the agriculture-based nobility. They were the capitalists at an epoch when capitalism in Russia was taking over from a pre-industrial society. Taking over with such speed, moreover, that the 'Merchants' had not had the time to change their name, which no longer corresponded to reality. They were 'Merchants' only because they belonged to the Merchant 'Estate', just as some factory workers were 'peasants' because they belonged to the peasant 'Estate', or some peasants were 'nobles' because they belonged to the 'Estate' of the Nobility. Within their own class-conscious hierarchy the social pride of place among 'Merchants' was held by those who in the West would have been called industrialists or factory owners or railway developers − Russia's Rockefellers, Vanderbilts, Astors, Fords, whom in many ways they resembled. Merchants in the true sense, trading in goods they had not themselves produced, were definitely second-rankers in social esteem, while on the lowest rung of all stood the man who in the current phrase 'made his money work for him', i.e. derived a higher income from interest on his loans to other 'merchants' than from the sale of his goods, if, indeed, he had any goods to sell. The somewhat scathing nickname for him was 'interest-man', *protsentshchik*.

Some 'merchants', by accepting a civilian decoration, a title or a nominal civil service rank, joined the ranks of the nobility, but on the whole this was never an ambition among them. They were too sure of their place in the world, too much aware of their rising power and of their contribution to their country's development to wish for a change in status.

Most of Russia's 'merchants', as of America's, came into prominence in the nineteenth century. Some of them came from trading families, but mostly they came from peasant stock, many of them religious dissenters. Some, like the Morozovs − the kings of them all − had been serfs, had made money by petty trading, founded factories and textile mills and then bought their freedom from their masters, sometimes − if the master happened to be greedy or difficult − for sums equivalent to thousands of pounds. They were a hard, ruthless lot, many of them, patriarchal, hard working, hard drinking, hard praying. Timofey Morozov, Russia's leading textile manufacturer, railway magnate, banker, whose father had founded the family's fortune, was a stern and exacting taskmaster, feared by his sons and his workmen alike. Yet he spent his nights on his knees, praying God to forgive him his harsh treatment of his employees. He knew of no other way of dealing with men in this world, but did not wish to jeopardize his chances in the next.

Others were more convivial. Mikhail Korolyov, highly respected Mayor of Moscow, would go to a pub with half a dozen of his cronies, 'merchants' like himself, put his top hat on the table and order champagne. The corks would be thrown into the hat. When the hat was full to the brim the friends would get up, pay, and calmly return to their respective offices apparently none the worse for wear.

Such gargantuan appetites for food and (especially) drink spilled over into lavish hospitality. According to those who could make the comparison, Siberian merchants were quite exceptional in this respect: it was considered a sign of meanness if the table-cloth was allowed to show through on a table laden with food and drink for a party; vodka was consumed by the yard (by individual guests in terms of glasses placed tightly next to each other) and so were pancakes — the Russians' favourite food at Carnival time.

Stories such as these have entered into the folklore of Russian 'merchant' life, together with the image of the typical merchant as a man of old-fashioned views and virtues (if any), conservative in dress, opinions, and way of life, a philistine interested in nothing but business, money, and the strict observance of church rites, a tyrant at home and at work. And after due allowance for an element of myth and exaggeration, such he probably remained as often as not, in far-off corners and remote provinces of the Empire till the very end of the nineteenth century and the early days of the twentieth. A typical specimen of this sort was a man of distinctive appearance, wearing a beard, his hair fairly long and cut so as to hang just below the nape of the neck. Usually he wore a peaked cap and was dressed in a long caftan with a stand-up collar hooked at the throat and baggy trousers tucked into top boots. Occasionally, though this was admittedly rare and becoming rarer, he was illiterate and transacted an astounding amount of business — very big business, some of it — by word of mouth, without bothering to record agreements on paper or signing them. Quite literally, his word was his bond.

However, this picture of him, though still a popular cliché, began to change with startling rapidity in the latter half of the nineteenth century when it became increasingly difficult to speak of 'the merchants' as a class or even as a homogeneous group or, indeed, as 'merchants'; 'industrialists' would have defined them better. Sharp and sharpening differences in the scale and nature of business enterprise, in income and education produced corresponding differences in manners and habits, attitudes and ways of life. As in other countries in transition from an agricultural to an industrial economy, Russia's social structure was breaking up. The tradition of *noblesse oblige* was, in John Bowlt's phrase, being replaced by *richesse oblige*, and the upper reaches of 'merchant' society led the way, probably more so in Moscow than elsewhere. The patronage of the arts was taken over by the new class of business tycoons, and their achievement is best, but by no means exhaustively, recalled to this day by the Moscow Art Theatre and the Tretyakov Gallery, named after its founder and familiar to every tourist in Moscow.

It would be manifestly untrue to say that but for them the Russian cultural renaissance of the nineteen hundreds would not have taken place, but it was certainly immensely facilitated by their encouragement. It was a constructive and discriminating encouragement, relying on the patron's own taste, ability and flair and not, as so often happened in the West at about the same time, on experts' and middlemen's advice. Indeed, the textile millionaire, Sergei Shchukin, specialized in 'rejected' artists and his immense collection of French Impressionists and Cubists, which influenced Russian art perhaps more profoundly than any other single factor and became a place of pilgrimage for foreign tourists and experts alike, was frequently made in the teeth of expert advice, when artists like Braque and Picasso were almost totally unknown. In the same way, Chagall found his first patron in Ivan Morozov (1871–1921) when he was still, and with no overwhelming success, struggling for recognition.

This independence of judgement and reliance on their own initiative was, of course, part of the nature of these highly successful businessmen, which led them and their families from poverty to riches. Typical, too, in this context is the story of Savva Morozov's involvement with the Moscow Art Theatre. Timofey Morozov's eldest son and by now head of the family and of the firm, the largest textile enterprise in Russia, Savva (1862–1905) was approached for funds to help the newly-founded Moscow Art Theatre. He immediately agreed and in his enthusiasm for the theatre he became its chief electrician, assistant producer, and part-architect: the new premises were built not only at his expense, but in accordance with his design, a conception of great originality.

The contribution of the wealthy Alexeyev family to that theatre was even greater, though not so tangible. The idea of it was conceived by Konstantin Alexeyev and Vladimir Nemirovich-Danchenko in 1897. It was opened the following year and Alexeyev became M.A.T.'s most influential director and producer (at no cost to the theatre, since neither he nor his actress wife received any salary). He is best known to the world under his assumed name: Stanislavsky.

Another typical characteristic of this 'merchant' patronage was the family nature of it. Every one of the five Shchukin brothers had an extensive collection of his own of pictures, books, furniture, arts and crafts, with the eldest, Sergei (1851–1936), branching out in directions other than art and becoming the founder of the Institute of Philosophy at Moscow University. Savva Mamontov (1841–1918), while promoting modern Russian painting, had two opera companies (though not concurrently) with guest artists such as Masini, Tamagno, and Chaliapine; his wife made the family estate, Abramtsevo, into a centre of Russian arts and crafts in which she was particularly interested, his son collected furniture and became a furniture designer.

But perhaps, as in so many respects, the palm should go to the Morozov family, the richest of all Russian industrialists, with the greatest ramifica-tion of interests in both business and intellectual activities. Varvara Morozov, herself the daughter of a textile magnate, Khludov, who, together with his brother built up an important collection of Russian manuscripts, books, and contemporary Russian pictures, had a political *salon* which flourished at the end of the nineteenth century and in the nineteen hundreds, probably the most important one in Moscow at that period. At the same time, her literary interests led her to found Moscow's first public library (the Turgenev library) and to pioneer schemes for workers' education. Her sons Michael (1870–1904) and Ivan (1871–1921) each built up vast collections of French impressionists, while Michael's wife Margarita, Scriabin's pupil and a very gifted pianist, was editor of the foremost Russian religio-philosophical journal 'The Way' ('*Put*' '). Her house was the meeting place of the Soloviev Philosophical Society, the members of which were, among others, Berdyaev, Bulgakov, and the Trubetskoy brothers.

The 1900s witnessed the heyday of these colourful representatives of the Russian bourgeoisie. They were amassing vast fortunes, they were spending these fortunes with a *panache* which, far from being useless, was enriching their country culturally and intellectually, and yet some other force within them was driving them on to will, or at least contribute to, their own destruction. It is a curious fact that so many of them, while creating their business empires, accumulating possessions, building imposing, indeed palatial, mansions, were at the same time surreptitiously, but none the less effectively and energetically, helping the forces whose avowed object was to dispossess them. As in all else, they succeeded admirably, and even here the Morozovs were in the forefront. Savva Morozov, the head of the family, became at an early age convinced of the truth of Marxism and the supporter of the Russian Social-Democratic (later renamed – Communist) Party, for reasons not, perhaps, very profound, but typical for a man of his stamp. What attracted him in Marxism, he said, was its practical approach to revolution, its energy. When in 1903 the Party split in two – the Bolsheviks under Lenin and the Mensheviks under Martov – he unhesitatingly chose the former: extremism, he thought, was natural for Russians and Lenin's methods promised to be effective. 'All Lenin's writings', he once remarked admiringly, 'could be entitled "A course in political face punching" '. His help to Lenin and his Party was severely practical: concealing in his sumptuous palace propaganda literature and Party members on the run from the police, and, above all, money. He financed Party activities, individual Party members, the Party press. Lenin's periodical, *Iskra* ('The Spark'), was kept alive, in great part, by Morozov's donations. Lenin's, or, indeed, the Communist Party's attitude to this generous helper of the coming revolution is not known, perhaps never will be. In 1905, after a quarrel with his mother over the management of his firm, he went to the French Riviera and shot himself in a hotel bedroom.

In the following year Morozov's nephew, N. P. Schmidt, ended in the same way – by committing suicide. Like his uncle he was an admirer of Lenin and a generous purveyor of funds to him and his organization, something he was able to accomplish after inheriting a large fortune both from his Morozov mother and from his father, a wealthy furniture manufacturer. Unlike his uncle, however, he was a full member of the Social-Democratic Party. The split between the Party's Bolshevik and Menshevik factions led to difficulties in apportioning the legacy, but the legacy nevertheless enabled the Bolsheviks, who got most if not all of it, to cope with their current financial troubles and to develop their activities.

The Soviet Encyclopaedia does not mention Morozov's name. It has, however, an article on the Tikhomirnov family, their communist affiliations, the posts occupied by the Tikhomirnovs in the early Bolshevik government and 'the active part taken by Victor Tikhomirnov at Lenin's behest in preparing the publication of *Pravda*'. There is no way of guessing from all this that the Tikhomirnovs were millionaire shipowners or that Victor Tikhomirnov founded *Pravda* in 1912 on his own initiative and supported it financially as he did other activities of Lenin's Party.

Why did he? Why did any of them, builders, like him, of Russia's emergent capitalist system? They were perfectly well aware of the fate that awaited them, their families and their possessions if the party and the men they so assiduously and so generously patronized, were to triumph. It

was, after all, as if Henry Ford, Mellon, the Astors, the Vanderbilts had been busily, if surreptitiously, financing the Communist Party of the United States. Can it be that these Russian merchants, descendants of a long line of religious dissenters, were unconsciously emulating their distant ancestors? In the seventeenth and even the eighteenth centuries these men, in protest against Church and State, would barricade themselves in their wooden houses, set fire to them, and perish in the flames, together with their wives, their children and their worldly goods. Can it be that the responses of their twentieth-century descendants to twentieth-century pressures consisted in a twentieth-century version of that self-immolation? Perhaps. Certainly the pressures had the same basic cause: alienation from State and Society produced by religion in one case, and by ideology – its twentieth-century surrogate – in the other.

Of all religions professed in the Russian Empire the Orthodox Church, including the schismatic or dissenting variety, claimed by far the greatest number of adherents: about two-thirds of the total population. In other words about as many as there were Russians (including Ukrainians, and Belorussians), in Russia. The adherents of other religions, though citizens of the Empire, were not ethnically Russian. In order of numerical importance they were Tartars and the Turkic tribes of Central Asia (Muslim); Poles (Catholic); Jews; Finns, Estonians, Latvians, Germans (Lutheran); Bashkirs and other Mongol tribes (Buddhist) etc.

For centuries the two concepts of Church and nationality had been not so much intertwined as merged in the Russian mind when applied to the Russians themselves. To say 'Orthodox' was to say 'Russian', and a Russian who was not also an Orthodox would have been unthinkable, a hybrid without a name. Indeed, to this day the Russian word for 'peasant' (and few indeed were not peasants right up to the twentieth century) is *krestyánin*, a scarcely corrupted form of *khristyanín* – a Christian, a synonym, in Russian eyes, for Orthodox.

The average Russian – peasant or townsman – could hardly visualize life without the ministrations and ceremonies of the Church. At his birth he would be baptized and a cross would be hung

The old Russian merchant class, conservative and religious often to eccentricity, had little in common
with a Western commercial bourgeoisie, at least until the late nineteenth century.
Here is an old-fashioned merchant family from the Nizhny Novgorod area: the men with long coats
and antique top hats and haircuts, the women in the brilliantly coloured silks
and brocades of traditional costume. One might wish to place this group, perhaps of an Old Believer family,
earlier than c. 1900 but one precisely dated 1905 is little different.

round his neck either on that day or later, never to be taken off again for the rest of his life. It was worn directly on the skin, never outside on one's shirt or dress, often with medallions or miniature icons attached. 'You've no cross on you' is (or was) the Russian way of saying 'You ought to be ashamed of yourself.' On baptism the child was given a saint's name (one only). His 'nameday' or 'Angel's day', as the Russians called it, i.e. the festival of his titular saint, would thereafter be celebrated annually in preference to his birthday (except, perhaps, among the westernized upper classes) generally by attendance at church, and greetings were sent to all friends and relations on appropriate saint's days.

Religion, or at least, public manifestations of it, intruded on every-day life to a degree far greater than in Western Europe. Peasants sowed and ploughed, reaped and mowed, remembered events and made plans by reference to the calendar of saints and church festivals – not just Christmas or Easter or Whitsun, but St Peter's Day and Our Lady's Intercession and the Annunciation and the Assumption and a host of saints, each with his or her own significance. In almost all houses, shops, restaurants, government offices, railway stations there were icons hanging high up in room corners, often with a small oil lamp burning in front of them. In villages at Christmas, Epiphany, and Easter the priest visited every house and held a short service; a service, too, would invariably be held in a newly occupied house by its new inhabitants; the many fasts were fairly rigorously kept, at least by the peasants; the other classes and town dwellers generally were less devout.

It must be admitted that Orthodox fasts are no light undertaking. Not only do they impose total abstinence from all animal produce, whether milk, butter, eggs or meat, but they outnumber all the other days of the year. Even the Catholics' one fast-day a week – Friday – is doubled to include Wednesday as well. Then there are the five weeks of St Peter's Fast ending on 29 June; the Fast of the Assumption lasting a fortnight, till 15 August; the Christmas Fast, another six weeks until Christmas Eve; and finally the longest of all, the Great Fast as the Russians call it, the seven weeks of Lent. This was the one fast conscientiously kept by all classes of the population. It culminates in Easter, the festival of festivals for

the Orthodox. The incessant services during Lent, particularly during Passion Week, the confession and Communion to which most Orthodox went, the total abstinence from food on Good Friday, all helped to build up a tension that found its dramatic release at the Easter Service which started on Saturday night two hours before midnight and finished with Mass in the early hours of Easter Sunday – a real test of endurance since at Orthodox services the congregation never sits: people either stand or kneel.

The Easter service begins in a church only dimly lit by candles flickering in front of icons. The singing is in a minor key, low and subdued, and there is an atmosphere of expectancy and almost of strain. Then, shortly before midnight, every member of the congregation lights a candle and, if he so wishes, joins a procession, which leaves the church with icons and banners and walks round it headed by the priest and deacons. At the stroke of midnight the church doors are flung open, the priest appears on the threshold and proclaims loudly and distinctly: 'Christ is risen!', to which he receives the response of the congregation: 'He is risen indeed!' The choir, in a triumphant canticle of Easter, takes up the theme of the Resurrection and every member of the congregation turns to his or her neighbour and kisses them three times, with the words 'Christ is risen!' and receives the answer: 'He is risen indeed!' (The kissing, it may be added in parenthesis, lasts the whole of Easter Week. Friends and simple acquaintances abandon the ritual of shaking hands and greet each other in houses and in the streets with the three-fold kiss, accompanied by the sacramental phrase.)

During Easter Week, rejoicing, the feeling of liberation from the constrictions and austerities of Lent, were genuine and surprisingly universal, sincerely religious, but encouraged by copious food and drink (for those who could afford it), particularly welcome after the long fast, and even more, perhaps, by the first intimations of spring, the thrillingly sudden revival of life after the long and bitter winter.

Orthodox services do not, as a rule, demand the active participation of the faithful in their celebration, such as singing hymns or making responses. They are conducted in Slavonic, a language sufficiently near Russian to be intelligible to listeners and yet sufficiently different to sound solemn and stately. No instrumental music is allowed, and the beauty of the service depends on the choir and on the deacon who has to sing his prayers and responses. A deacon with a good bass voice was sometimes given a musical education and training as a singer, was invited to sing (secular as well as church music) in private homes and had his *aficionados* and partisans in exactly the same way as Chaliapine or any other great artist.

Choirs were held in even higher esteem and there was keen rivalry between them. Even private, non-ecclesiastical institutions had choirs trained to sing in church. As befits private enterprise, competition among them was particularly strong. Sometimes, it seems, at the expense of business efficiency. Thus one bank manager was known to select his clerks with a single criterion in mind: their singing proficiency. *His* church choir was to be the best at whatever cost to more material considerations.

Churches famous for their deacons and their choirs attracted large congregations, which found their religious emotions greatly enhanced by aesthetic appreciation. This aesthetic appreciation is much in the tradition of the Russian Church. Russia is probably the only country in the world to claim that its adoption of its religious faith was originally due to reasons which were neither ethical nor spiritual and which concerned themselves with neither truth nor grace. They were, according to the old chonicle, entirely aesthetic: the Russians, it seems, had been seduced by the beauty of the Orthodox ritual they had witnessed in Constantinople and as they stood in the great church of St Sophia, 'knew not whether [they] were in heaven or on earth'. They, therefore, chose the Orthodox religion in preference to any other – whether Catholic, Muslim or Jewish – because, they said, 'any man who has tasted something sweet is thereafter unwilling to accept that which is bitter'.

To this ritual, which they adopted at the end of the tenth century and which seemed to them so superior to any other, the Russians have remained passionately faithful, and when in the seventeenth century the Russian Patriarch introduced slight changes in the form of the service and in sacerdotal gestures and improved the translation of the Scriptures, it was enough to split the Russian Orthodox Church into two hostile groups, which have never become reconciled: the schismatics or Old Believers (they preferred to call themselves Old Ritualists) clung to the original ritual, while the Established Church adopted the reforms and enjoyed official favour and protection. This did not save it, however, from its administration being radically changed by Peter the Great in the eighteenth century, when the Patriarchate was abolished and an office known as the Holy Synod set up in its stead. Its *de facto* ruler (under the Emperor) became a lay official with the rank of Chief Procurator.

The pot-bellied priest, sleek and well-fed, striding disdainfully among his famished and ragged parishioners is a familiar cliché of Soviet cartoons, but in real life he would have been an unusual sight. Financially he was hardly, if at all, better off than the peasants around him. Not, as a rule, paid a salary by the State, he depended for his living on whatever his parishioners agreed to pay him after some haggling, for weddings, funerals, and christenings, and – if he was a village priest – on the produce from a few acres of glebe land which he often cultivated himself, following his plough like any of his parishioners. Socially his position was not a happy one. The upper and middle classes looked down on him because of his inferior status, his poverty, his low educational standard; the intelligentsia prided itself on being rational and, even more, on being atheist and, therefore, treated him with contempt and saw (or pretended to see) in him nothing but a government agent and a hypocritical tool of the possessing classes; the peasants, so often at loggerheads with him over church dues, suspected or accused him of being mean and grasping, failing to realize that without these dues he and his family would be unable to survive.

His situation, difficult as it was, was made worse by the absence of any possibility of improving his lot by promotion beyond the modest status of archpriest. Bishoprics were beyond his grasp since these went exclusively to monks. The Russian clergy was divided into so-called 'White' and 'Black'. The parish priest belonged to the first. He was usually himself descended from a long line of parish priests, and his surname, often

A group of skhimniki, *hermits of the most zealous kind, who followed a very strict rule of monasticism.*
Those standing have passed all their vows, their habits
show the instruments of the martyrdom of Christ and a text from Luke 9 : 24.

derived from some Church festival, bore witness to this. His speech, studded with church Slavonic, and his special ecclesiastical accent which he learned in the seminary and heard at home, would have made him instantly recognizable even without his cassock or his beard and long hair which he was not allowed to cut. He was obliged to marry before ordination — for no unmarried man could be ordained unless he was a monk — and usually chose a girl from an ecclesastical family similar to his own. But should his wife die, he was not allowed to marry again. He could, however, become a monk and thus join the ranks of the 'Black' clergy to which alone high preferment was open. From their ranks came bishops, archbishops, and metropolitans.

Monks and, indeed, the whole institution of monasticism have had their critics no less in Russia than elsewhere; perhaps more in Russia since Orthodox monasticism is a contemplative rather than active institution and was, therefore, attacked as useless and costly: there were in Russia no teaching or nursing orders, and monasteries were by no means centres of learning. But whatever the merits and defects of Russia's innumerable monasteries and convents, they fulfilled one apparently vital need of the Russian nature – the need to wander. Historically, the expansion of the Empire was due to a great extent to that innate Russian *wanderlust*. The monasteries attracted thousands of pilgrims who, barefoot and in rags, begged their way over vast distances to worship at a venerated shrine or icon, or to seek advice and consolation from a *starets*, an elder. The *startsy* (plural of *starets*) were men, whether in holy orders or not, reputed for their wisdom and holy life, who led an anchoritic existence often in or near a monastery, but sometimes entirely alone in some remote forest. Their primary role was to save themselves, but others hoped to be saved by their example and advice.

Side by side with the Established Orthodox Church, the schismatic Old Ritualists continued to exist, to prosper and to increase. In some ways they could be compared – with due allowance for national character and social structure — to British Nonconformists, not only for their modest social origins (they were mainly peasants), but also for their great regard for the simple virtues. They were abstemious, honest, hard-working and, as a result, more prosperous, on the average, than their neighbours. They contributed greatly to the rise of the bourgeoisie and, with the upswing of Russia's economic development in the nineteenth century, founded some of the great merchant dynasties of Moscow. In matters of religion they were bigoted and narrow-minded, so fearful of being contaminated by men of other faiths (particularly the Established Church) that some of them carried their own forks and spoons with them to minimize contact with the abominable heretics by not sharing their cutlery at mealtimes.

Paradoxically, this ultra-conservative dissent, springing from an exaggerated concern for ritualism, promoted its direct opposite — proliferation of sects preaching and practising spiritual freedom unshackled by ecclesiastical rules and dogma. The original seventeenth-century revolt against ecclesiastical authority and the refusal to comply with the teaching – if only in matters of ritual — of the Established Church, released the latent popular protest against constraints of any kind. Some sects, it is true, were extravagant and grotesque, and much attention has been focused on them for that reason. There were the *Skoptsý* (Self-Castrators), for instance, who believed in total sexual abstinence, but clearly could not trust themselves to achieve it without surgical assistance; the *Khlystý*, who also believed in sexual abstinence, but only between husband and wife – other people's husbands and wives were, thoughtfully, excluded from the ban, and concubinage was encouraged (as well as abortion); the Holy Ghost Worshippers, who had to breathe in deeply at prayer time, in the hope of swallowing the Third Person of the Trinity. That success was not without its attendant dangers is shown by the case of the famous nineteenth-century Russian portrait painter Borovikovsky, member of the sect. He collapsed during one of these deep-breathing sessions and died — according to his co-religionists – of surfeit of Holy Ghost. An enviable death, no doubt.

However, all these oddities were probably less important and had fewer adherents than the perfectly respectable Evangelical, Baptist, and Methodist-type groups that began to spread very rapidly at the end of the nineteenth century in spite of Government persecution and all the restrictions placed on conversion to their faith.

It seems to have been generally accepted that, but for these restrictions, half the Russian peasants would have gone over to the Old Ritualists and other sectarians. Unfortunately, there was no acceptable official estimate of their number, since they successfully evaded registration in most cases. The 1897 census put the combined total number of Old Ritualists and sectarians at 2.2 million, but the actual figure was authoritatively estimated at nearer 20 million, and at about 25 million (including 6 million sectarians) by the beginning of World War I.

Perhaps the greatest weakness of the Russian Orthodox Church was the alienation from it of the intelligentsia, particularly during the latter half of the nineteenth century. Partly this was, of course, the Church's own fault: its deficiencies were glaring enough even to churchmen. But more important, and certainly enough to damn it in the eyes of the intelligentsia, was the fact that it had official status and enjoyed the patronage and support of the State. Besides, atheism was almost a tenet of unquestioned faith in progressive intellectual circles and any compromise on that score would have been interpreted by them as treason. All the more remarkable was the revolution in religious thought which took place at the beginning of the twentieth century when some of the country's leading intellectuals – Berdyayev, Bulgakov, Frank, Merezhkovsky among others – abandoned the fashionable materialistic outlook of the time and not only proclaimed the primacy of spiritual values, but sought the expression of these values in the Established Church. All that was needed, according to them, was a reinterpretation of the Church's teaching, not least by the Church itself. Partly under the influence of its new-found allies, partly in answer to pressures within itself, the Orthodox Church by the end of the Tsarist regime was gradually entering on a period of reform which was interrupted by the Revolution, the persecution of the Church and the resultant entirely new relationship between it and the State.

This new, post-Revolution, relationship was only part of the State's altered attitude to religion as such and therefore to all religions within its borders. The ideal became to abolish religion altogether and hence to secularise all activities, including education, which could lead to its main-tenance or revival. The difficulties of secularization in communities such as the Muslims and the Jews, where religion had penetrated all aspects of life, particularly education, were indeed formidable, and in the case of Jews could be, or at least could be interpreted as, another form of anti-Semitism – an understandably sensitive point in the love-hate relationship of Jews and Russians.

It is a curious fact of history that the Jews, so numerous in Russia, did not, for the most part, come to that country. It was Russia that came to them. The annexation of the Ukraine in the seventeenth century and, even more, the partition of Poland in the eighteenth, turned Russia almost overnight from a country with a numerically negligible Jewish population into one with the highest number of Jews in the world and rapidly increasing. At the beginning of Nicholas II's reign the Jewish community in the Russian Empire only just exceeded five million. Twenty years later they numbered about seven million in spite of a million and a quarter emigrants in the same period of time making their way abroad – chiefly to America – to escape poverty and persecution. By far the largest of Russia's ethnic minorities except the Poles, it was also one of the most remarkable for the vigour and – in spite, or, perhaps, because, of constant harassment – the independence of its communal life, the number and calibre of its spiritual leaders and its contribution to the country's cultural, political, and economic development.

The last two decades of the Empire's existence were the time of the flowering of a specifically Jewish culture in Russia. Both Hebrew in its modernized form and Yiddish were being fashioned as languages of literature – mainly (some would say, entirely) by Russian Jews in Russia. The first can boast of having produced three truly great Hebrew poets – Bialik (1873–1934), a native of Odessa, perhaps the greatest of all modern Hebrew poets and certainly the best known internationally; Saul Tchernichowsky and Zalman Schneur, who still await their translators. Russo-Jewish composers sometimes used libretti written in Yiddish for opera on Jewish themes. At the turn of the century L. S. Lwu's 'The Queen of Jerusalem' and Lustgarten's 'The Oath in the Temple' were particularly popular with Jewish audiences in

Russia. More serious — and certainly more literary — writers in Yiddish (Sholom Aleichem, Sholem Ash, Mendele, Peretz are probably the best known names) tried to throw a bridge from the exclusive and traditional, almost theocratic, world of Jewry concentrated in the Pale of Settlement, and the secular and more open society which surrounded it and was luring the younger generation away from it.

The younger generation was increasingly keen to be lured away and take part in the life of Russia as a whole. In the world of literature the first Russian Jew to have gained renown and popularity with the Russian public was Minsky (pseudonym of N. M. Vilenkin, 1855–1937). (Nadson, whose popularity was even greater, was his contemporary, but Nadson was not recognized by the Jewish community, since his mother was a Gentile.) To modern ears Minsky's poetry sounds somewhat spineless and trite, but the aestheticism and mysticism which he cultivated in the 1880s and 1890s marked the beginning of the Russian Modernist movement of which he may be considered as one of the founders. Together with Merezhkovsky he started the Religious and Philosophic Society, and was one of the precursors of the Symbolists. Once the first step was taken, the Russian Jews soon found themselves in the forefront of Russian cultural development.

In the last few years of the Imperial regime Russo-Jewish poets and prose writers such as Pasternak, Mandelstam and Babel made their appearance — a far cry from Minsky in sheer literary quality; Chagall, Bakst, the Burliuk brothers, Naum Gabo, Anton Pevsner, and a host of others were taking part in the revival — 'the Great Experiment', as it has been aptly called — of Russian art; Semyon Frank and Lev Shestov (Schwarzmann) were adding to the (admittedly meagre) achievements of Russian philosophy, and Russian literary criticism and historical writing were greatly enriched by Shklovsky, Gershenzon, and others. In the sphere of music (performers and teachers — violinists in particular — rather than composers) the Russo-Jewish contribution was so distinguished and so obvious that it is almost superfluous to mention it. Besides, more perhaps than in any other sphere of art, it made itself felt not only in Russia, but throughout the world. Auer, Mischa Elman, Anton Rubinstein, Kous-

sevitsky, Heifetz, Horowitz were (and still are) household names on an international level, yet they are a mere handful taken almost at random. A really representative list would be too long.

Russia's rapid economic expansion during that period would possibly not have been quite as spectacular without the Jewish financiers, shipping and railway magnates, industrialists and merchants of the stature of Baron Günzburg, Polyakov, Visotsky, the dynasty of the Brodsky sugar 'kings', to name but a very few, since the Jews made up over a third of Russia's total trading community. Gold mining and the two key economic activities of Russia — timber and the grain trade — were to a very considerable extent concentrated in Jewish hands, and the same was true of such diverse industries as flour milling, textiles, leather, tobacco, and beer brewing.

In any town, big or small, in Western Russia such essential members of the community as tailors, shoemakers, glaziers, cabinet makers, dispensing chemists were often, perhaps even generally, Jews, and in South-West Russia — particularly in Poland and Ukraine — the pub keepers were Jewish almost to a man. Peasants depended largely on Jewish middlemen for the sale of their produce and to put them in touch with suppliers of necessities — groceries, agricultural implements etc. The Jewish pedlar was a familiar figure, basically welcome because indispensable, though his physical appearance, his accent, his faulty or peculiar Russian, his clothes, his manner cut him off sharply from his customers and made for a social gulf which neither side wanted to cross.

Yet, in spite of a culturally and economically influential Jewish *élite* and a fairly prosperous bourgeoisie, the great mass of the Jewish people in Russia lived in penury rendered all the more difficult to bear by legal disabilities and by an insecurity highlighted by inter-communal strife, the 'pogroms', when the authorities not only failed adequately to protect Jewish citizens against attack by their Gentile neighbours, but were accused of having, on occasion, fomented the pogroms themselves. The legal disabilities, however, were based on religious and in no way on racial discrimination. They did not apply to sectarian Jews, such as the Karaites (living mostly in the Crimea), who did not accept the Talmud, or to the so-called Mountain Jews in the Caucasus, strongly tainted with paganism and speaking their own Judeo-Tat dialect, or to Jews in Central Asia (Turkestan), regarded by the Russian authorities as part of the native population, as, indeed, they were, or to Jews who allowed themselves to be baptized and were received into a Christian Church of whatever denomination. No distinction whatsoever was made between them and the Gentile population, Christian or Muslim.

For Orthodox Jews the legal disabilities meant, first and foremost, their virtual exclusion (at least according to the letter of the law) from all parts of the Empire outside the Pale of Settlement – the area comprising mainly Eastern Poland, Lithuania, Ukraine, and Bessarabia, where Russian conquest or annexation had originally found them. Permission to live permanently outside that area was given only to a minority: to old-established communities, as in the Baltic provinces, the Caucasus and Central Asia as well as to Siberian colonists and to certain specific categories, such as domestic servants, artisans, all university graduates (and, therefore, professional men such as doctors and lawyers), members of the First Merchant Guild and – in practice – the more important businessmen, industrialists, bankers (and, of course, the families of all these categories). And to prostitutes.

But even these were subjected to various restrictions such as the imposition of a percentage quota for prospective grammar school (*gimnaziya*) and State university entrants, though it should in fairness be added that many, particularly among the more traditional elements, preferred to keep their children away from Gentile educational establishments for fear of their being contaminated by an alien religion and alien customs. Families were split on that very sore subject and family dramas were a common occurrence. The eminent Jewish-Russian lawyer, Genrikh Sliozberg, never forgot the 'real grief' of his family and relatives when they discovered that his father had sent him to a Russian grammar school. His school uniform they found particularly irritating, sinful even. It was, they thought, 'an apostate's garb', and his mother and grandmother cried bitterly every time they saw him in it.

Fortunately, strict observance of the law has never been the Russian *forte*. In the case of Jewish residence legislation requiring the expulsion of unauthorized Jews back to the Pale of Settlement, full and literal compliance would have been disastrous to both parties. It would have meant the permanent expulsion of people absolutely indispensable to the normal working of life in the community. The law was, therefore, often either ignored or circumvented, or else expulsion was followed by a gradual seeping back of at least some of the expellees or of their co-religionists. It was not a satisfactory solution, it produced a great deal of human misery and, at best, inconvenience and uncertainty, but it mitigated what would otherwise have been an untenable situation. In the same way, school and university quotas were not strictly adhered to, but their very existence obviously rankled and in any case constituted a threat and an additional obstacle to a normal career.

The bulk of the Orthodox Jews, three-quarters of them artisans or petty traders, living within the Pale of Settlement, were even there restricted mainly to urban centres where they formed on average two-fifths, and in Belorussia and Lithuania over half, of the population. In some towns they formed the overwhelming majority. Seldom speaking anything but Yiddish, unable for the most part either to read or write in Russian, they were immersed entirely in their own culture, observed faithfully and minutely the precepts of their religion and their customs, and sent their sons to their own schools – the Kheders and the Yeshivahs – to learn Hebrew, the Bible, and the Talmud. The Russian-Jewish revolutionary, Lev Deutsch, writing in 1923, clearly remembered the time when the Jews 'considered it sinful to learn Russian, and its use was allowed only if absolutely essential and, of course, only for speaking to Christians (the *goyim*)'. Even the clothes they wore set them apart from the rest of the population, though the distinctive robes and hats, often redolent of the Middle Ages, if in a sense typical, were worn only by a minority: the rabbis and the religious élite.

Of course conditions varied. In Russian Poland and in Lithuania the Jews were stricter and more exclusive, adhered more closely to their customs, led a life of greater religious intensity than in Ukraine or Bessarabia. They were famous for their rabbis and religious teachers whose advice was sought, quoted, and (sometimes) followed through-

Aged orthodox Jew reading the early morning prayers read every day by the religious.
The box attached to his forehead and another to his left arm (not visible under the tallit, or prayer shawl)
contain scriptural texts, and are known as tefillin (phylacteries).

out Jewry. In Ukraine, on the other hand, the Jews mixed more freely with the Gentile population and were gradually abandoning their own distinctive customs and even dress: most men did not wear caftans and skull caps otherwise than in the synagogue and even beards among them were by no means universal. Fewer and fewer girls cut their hair on marriage to wear a wig thereafter.

Towards the end of the period the world of Russian Jewish Orthodoxy was beginning to crack. The process of assimilation was rapidly gathering momentum – socially through increasing social intercourse and even intermarriage, and politically through an appeal to revolutionary internationalism. At the same time, religious and traditional exclusiveness was finding new expression either in secular political organizations such as the *Bund* ('General Jewish Workers' Union in Lithuania, Poland, and Russia'), claiming Jewish national and cultural autonomy within the Russian Empire, or in Zionism, aiming at total emigration and the creation of an independent Jewish State. The pressure to abolish the Pale of Settlement and with it all the other legal disabilities was growing both from the Jewish side, and from that of educated Russians. However, resistance from the more traditional elements continued strong enough to nullify not only the efforts of the largest Party in the Duma – the Cadets – but even the expressed wish of the strongest of the Imperial Prime Ministers, Stolypin. It was left to the Provisional Government, immediately after the abdication of the Emperor, to introduce the equality of all Russian citizens before the law.

But the Russo-Jewish culture which had attained considerable distinction and of which the Jews (and Russians, too) were so justly proud, did not long survive the fall of the Tsarist regime. It was, after all, the product of its time and of the circumstances which enabled it to develop and to flourish. After the fall of the Provisional Government and the seizure of power by the Communist Party, the more distinguished representatives of the Russo-Jewish intelligentsia joined the great exodus of Russian lawyers, writers, scientists, artists, musicians and other intellectuals to settle in other countries. At the same time, as a result of the partial break-up of the Russian Empire, well over half the Jewish population of Russia found itself living outside the borders of the newly-formed Union of Soviet Socialist Republics.

Viewed (as the Russians at the time emphatically did not view them) as a national or ethnic group, the Jews represented one of a vast number of minority peoples which made up the Russian Empire.

Indeed one of the most striking impressions that Russia made on any visitor was the variety of nationalities and races that jostled each other everywhere, differing in language, physical type, customs, manners, even in occupation. Thus waiters in restaurants were often Tartars, prized for their abstemiousness since their Muslim faith forbade them to drink alcohol; shoemakers and tailors were frequently Jews; Estonians and Baltic Germans, considered above average in honesty and education, were in great demand as factors and managers of estates – an important post since absenteeism was the rule among wealthy landowners; the building of flour mills was the speciality of Lettish artisans organized in itinerant co-operatives. And so on.

There were about 200 different nationalities living in this vast expanse of land almost nine million square miles in area – a quarter of it in Europe and the rest in Asia, stretching from the Baltic Sea to the Pacific Ocean, from the Arctic Circle to Afghanistan. Some of these nationalities formed no more than a few tribes or even groups of families, primitive and poor, hardly out of the stone age – like the Chukchi of Siberia; others, like the Poles, sophisticated and prosperous, with a great history of formerly independent existence and rich traditions behind them, claiming to have reached a higher cultural level and degree of political and economic development than the nation that exercised dominion over them. The dominant nation, the Great Russians, that is Russians without Ukrainians or Belorussians (admittedly not always a clear-cut distinction), made up less than half the total population. Over a quarter of that population was non-Slav and perhaps a fifth was not even Christian and belonged, with the obvious exception of the Jews, to a totally different culture, mainly Muslim, but also Buddhist as well as Pagan. The Muslims – some 20–25 million of them (the precise figure is disputed) – not only represented a formidable number, but were given cohesion by the existence on Russian territory of great centres of Islamic learning, such, for instance, as the city of Kazan, on the Volga, which yielded in this respect to no other city in the world except Cairo and Constantinople. All along the Volga, from Nizhny Novgorod (now Gorki) to Astrakhan on the Caspian, as well as in the Crimea on the Black Sea, lived the remnants of the Golden Horde, the erstwhile masters of Russia at the time of the 'Tartar Yoke'. Kazan and Astrakhan were conquered by the Russian Tsar in the sixteenth century and became the foundation stones of the Russian Empire and the prelude to its Eastward expansion. The Tartars of the Crimea, annexed two centuries later, continued to live undisturbed till Stalin's day, when they were uprooted and the survivors deported to Central Asia.

Before the Revolution, Central Asia was officially referred to as Turkestan and the Steppe Region, with a population of Turkmenians, Uzbeks, Kazakhs, Kurds, Afghans and others, all of them Muslims. It was Russia's most recent acquisition, and by the beginning of this century, in spite of great economic changes, the development of agriculture and of industry based on cotton, the expanding network of schools, everyday life in Turkestan had not changed much since the Russian conquest a quarter of a century previously. Men and women continued to follow their own customs and traditional occupations, to wear their national dress and live in their houses of clay and sun-baked brick if they belonged to a settled agricultural population, or in felt tents if they were members of a nomadic tribe following their cattle, camels, and horses from pasture to pasture.

However, the Russian population was increasingly infiltrating the newly acquired territory and by the end of the twentieth century's first decade reached about two million out of a total of over ten. The greater part of the Russian settlers – about two-thirds of them – were peasants who had come to Central Asia in search of land, had built their *izbas* in Russian-type villages and led a life entirely separate from the native population.

But the search for new land drove the Russian peasant not so much to the inhabited territories of Central Asia as to the empty spaces of Siberia. When at the end of the sixteenth century the

Russians pushed their way beyond the Urals they found a land almost devoid of inhabitants, only a few primitive tribes wandering up and down the vast wastes of Siberia – five million square miles of it. Three centuries later, with the native population at about a million, there were some nine million Russian settlers who had built towns and villages and begun the economic – mainly agricultural – development of the country. The native population had not changed much over that period of time. Either Pagan or Buddhist (with a few Muslims and nominal Christians), most of them by the beginning of the twentieth century were nomads, dependent on their herds of reindeer for food, clothing, shelter (tents), and transport. Some of them had only recently – within a generation or two – emerged from a stone-age culture and very few of them had learnt to speak Russian. As a rule these tribes had been left by the Russian authorities to their own devices; they were subject to their own law, professed their own religion and carried on their immemorial customs as they had always done. Up to the last years of the nineteenth century the Russian penetration of Siberia was more nominal than real – a few thousand convicts and political exiles, several hundred thousand inhabitants of rather unattractive, timber-built towns and some four million peasants. That was all.

The exiles and convicts dated from the earliest days of Russian penetration of Siberia – it was, in that sense, Russia's Australia. Among the first to suffer that fate, however, was neither a political dissenter nor a common criminal. It was a bell.

On 15 May 1591 the citizens of Uglich, a small city on the upper Volga, north of Moscow, were summoned to the main square by the tolling of the Cathedral bell announcing the death of the young Prince Dimitri, half-brother of the reigning Tsar. The rumour immediately spread that he had been murdered by the partisans of the Regent, Boris Godunov, who was waiting for the ailing and feeble-minded Tsar's death to seize the throne for himself – as he eventually did – and was, therefore, keen to eliminate the natural heir. The crowd, egged on by Boris's enemies, went on the rampage, killed the Prince's alleged murderers, and looted a few houses. A commission sent to Uglich duly reported that the Prince had inadvertently killed himself in an epileptic fit, and it blamed the Regent's ill-wishers for instigating the riot. And who had started the rioting? Why, the bell, of course, the great bell of the Cathedral, by calling out the people to the main square. The bell was clearly to blame and as the main culprit it was sentenced to be taken down and deported to the newly founded city of Tobolsk in Siberia to remain there forever in ignominy and shame.

In a sense, therefore, the bell of Uglich should be regarded as the patron of all Siberian exiles. But not of the main bulk of Siberia's Russian population which was made up of peasants, who, despite official disapproval (inspired by the fear of a possible labour shortage in European Russia) and attempts to bring them back, made their way beyond the Urals in search of more land and a better life or to escape the law, the authorities, religious persecution or their masters who owned them in the days of serfdom. They had to rely on their own initiative and toughness to get them through the dangers of a trek which lasted many months and sometimes years, to survive on the way and to begin a new existence in hard and unfamiliar surroundings. The casualties were enormous, but those who won through found themselves free and far more prosperous than they had ever been before.

However, by the 70s and 80s of the nineteenth century serfdom was a thing of the past and the climate of opinion began to change. Russian literature took up the cause of peasant settlers and romanticized them as heroes in the great saga of national expansion – the bid for freedom of simple men and women, who braved natural dangers and official disapproval to bring empty lands into cultivation and broaden their own and their country's horizons. The government, with some hesitation at first, not only recognized the futility of its attempt to put obstacles in the way of would-be settlers, but realized, too, the economic and political advantage of providing land-hungry peasants with millions of acres of rich, hitherto uncultivated soil. Its attitude switched from that of trying to make the peasants go back to European Russia, if possible in each case to their original village, to its precise opposite, until in the beginning of the present century its slogan became: 'Go East, young man – and take your village with you'. Prospective settlers were now allowed tax relief and were given direct grants in

land, livestock, money, and helped with technical advice. Transit camps and food centres were organized on the way from European Russia to points of settlement and – more important than any other single measure – the Trans-Siberian Railway was built, drastically shortening the time taken to complete the immense journey.

Even so it was no easy undertaking. The settlers would be faced with the necessity to build everything from scratch. They would start from constructing a sort of dug-out, 'something', says a contemporary official report, 'between a human dwelling and a beast's lair', little more than a hole in the ground covered with a roof. In a surprisingly short time, however, houses would be built and a village grow up, faithfully reproducing the type of architecture and lay-out of the settlers' home village – the long white-washed houses with thatched roofs of Southern Russia, the clay and wattle cottages of Ukraine, the log cabins of Central and North European Russia. And within six or seven years, sometimes much less, the average settler would be the owner of a farm four times the size of his old holding in European Russia, yielding a correspondingly higher income.

In the twenty years from the beginning of Nicholas II's reign to the eve of World War I, some four million men and women came, mainly as a result of the Government's efforts, to settle in Siberia – just about as many as had done in all the three preceding centuries – and of these, some three million crossed the Urals in the seven years 1907–13. The total population of Siberia had doubled in the course of these two decades and by 1914 had reached about $10\frac{1}{2}$ million, including nine million Russians, a million natives and half a million others. Siberia was taking off.

Russia beyond the Urals – Siberia and Turkestan – was the main area of Russia's Empire building, where its population was increasing by rapid colonization. The Caucasus, west of Central Asia, across the Caspian Sea, with its great mountains and magnificent scenery, attracted individuals and tourists – apart from officials and the army – rather than settlers, though these, too, came, if only in small numbers. Its valleys were too densely populated to admit many newcomers from outside. Besides, its 40–45 different tribes and nationalities, whether Christian like the Armenians and Georgians, or Muslim like most of

*A guard post on the Georgian Military Road. The sentry-box is striped black and white
with a narrow orange line separating the two colours.*

the Highlanders, were all fiercely individualistic
and proud of their long history of independence
and civilization stretching back to pre-Christian
times when they formed part of the Greco-Roman
world. Russia took about a century – mainly the
nineteenth – to subject them and weld them to
herself, partly through their voluntary submission
(as a protection against Turkey or Persia) and
partly by conquest and annexation, but each of
them preserved its own particular character, way
of life, dress, and language: 'Language Mountain'
was the medieval Arab historians' nickname for
the Caucasus.

A peculiar feature in Russia was the presence
of foreign minorities, some of which had originally

been invited or induced to come to Russia as a
group and had continued to lead their own separate existence unabsorbed by the surrounding
population and refusing to be assimilated. Such
were, for example, the Lithuanian Tartars already
mentioned in another connection (see p. 24);
such too the 'German colonists' on the Volga,
farmers whose arrival in Russia dated back to
Catherine II's time in the eighteenth century. At
the beginning of the twentieth century the bulk
of them still lived in a compact group on the same
lands, in well-furnished, solidly-built houses,
startlingly different from the *izbas* of the Russian
peasants, keeping their customs and even their
fashions (men clean-shaven, women in German,

sometimes eighteenth-century style, dresses), faithful to their Protestant religion, intermarrying among themselves, speaking nothing but German to each other, and Russian with a strong German accent only to their Russian neighbours. They were admired for their efficiency and left practically undisturbed until, in the course of the Second World War, they were deported and dispersed throughout Russia by Stalin's Government.

Dispersed, too, or allowed to go to Germany at the time of Stalin's annexation of Estonia, Latvia, and Lithuania in 1940, were the so-called Baltic Germans. Before the Revolution these States were Russian provinces in which Germans formed a minority within a minority. But only numerically. Economically, politically, culturally, and socially they dominated the native populations, and the towns had little to distinguish them, architecturally, from North German towns. Their upper class – the 'Baltic Barons' – considered themselves not so much Russian subjects as servants of the Emperor, bound to him by personal loyalty. Their stamping ground was the army, the Foreign Office, and the Court where they served without cutting their links with their Baltic background and interests. The native Baltic population was in the main agricultural. Culturally it was strongly influenced by Scandinavia.

This was particularly true of Finland, whose upper class was Swedish by origin and which occupied a special position within the Russian Empire. It was an independent Grand-Duchy under a Grand-Duke who was also Russian Emperor. It had a Constitution and a Parliament when Russia had neither – a Parliament, moreover, elected after 1906 by very nearly universal suffrage of both sexes, making Finland the first country in the world to give votes to women. It was governed under its own laws, had its own administration and educational system, and its citizens were not liable to serve in the Russian armed forces. At the turn of the century and again just before World War I, the Russian government tried to curtail Finnish autonomy and constitutional rights. But the attempt served only to drive the Finns into opposition and embitter the relations between the two countries.

With the largest of Russia's Baltic possessions, Poland, relations were not, and had never been, satisfactory. Poland remained a subjugated, but restive country, and the Russian attitude to it varied from acknowledging it as a separate entity, with its own Constitution and a Customs barrier, to treating it – as in the last reign – simply as an extension of Russian territory. In the former phase it was known as a 'Tsardom', whose Tsar was the Russian Emperor, bound by a Constitution not applicable to Russia itself. In the latter phase, the very name of Poland became suspect, and though never officially changed, the country was referred to in school books and official documents as the Vistula Region. It was not, it may be added, a designation ever used outside these official documents and school books, and the Emperor continued to be styled 'Tsar of Poland', though by now no longer bound by a special Polish Constitution.

Poland has often been called Russia's Ireland, and there was, indeed, a great deal in common in the relationship of these two countries with the dominant nation – the religious controversy, the historical conflict, the ruthlessness of domination. On the other hand, it had never been Great Britain's policy to develop Ireland's industry, whereas Poland became one of the more industrialized regions of the Russian Empire and had, on the whole, a higher standard of living than Russia itself. Besides, its Roman Catholicism drew it culturally into the Western orbit as much as the Orthodox Church linked Russia with the South-East of Europe. All this enhanced Poland's sense of cultural superiority over Russia and made it view Russia with a contempt embittered by the knowledge of its helplessness. Nevertheless, the Polish nobility continued sending their sons to Russian *élite* schools and Guards regiments, and accepted the highest posts in the Russian administration and at the Russian Court where they were much admired for their polished manners and their westernized elegance. Warsaw was regarded as a kind of Slav Paris, where Russian ladies with means to do so liked to order their dresses. To every Russian, Poland was, after all, 'Europe' – or very nearly. For to Russians 'Europe' was less a geographical fact than a cultural concept in which they never dreamt of including themselves. If they ever said about a compatriot that he was 'a European', they invariably meant it as a term of praise, connoting probity, good manners, education, and a reasonable attitude to life.

Education particularly. The urgent necessity of education was felt as the first priority – not education as the privilege of a few (they had that already), but as a natural heritage for all.

Education has such a different tradition and, therefore, meaning in Russia and England that one hesitates to use the same word for both. In England the original aim of education was to develop the individual; the idea that the school could also have a civic purpose came much later, though it is now being increasingly stressed. In Russia education has been from the very beginning, and particularly since Peter the Great, imposed by the State for its own ends (universities were regarded in the nineteenth century as merely training colleges for the civil service). That the real purpose of education was to develop the human personality for its own sake was regarded as a daring and original theory when it was first voiced at the end of the nineteenth century. But once voiced, it became the basis of all efforts by educational reformers (though not by all Ministers of Education) throughout the last reign.

Indeed, nothing was more typical of the Russian educational system in the beginning of the twentieth century than the feeling of urgency to reform it, the experimentation that went on with this end in view and the tension which pervaded it. The tension could in many ways be compared to the wave of unrest which, seventy years later, surged up in Western European educational establishments. In Western Europe, however, the wave subsided fairly quickly, at least in its more extreme manifestations. In Russia the unrest continued for decades (until snuffed out by the Revolution), and the more humdrum expressions of it, such as student and schoolchildren strikes, sit-ins, and demonstrations, were punctuated by more dramatic events, such as expulsions of university students by ministers of education and assassinations of ministers of education by university students. But apart from using force, the Government tried to cope with the situation by introducing reforms, devising new systems of education or curricula or types of school, by extending the network of educational establishments and by allowing private initiative to extend it too – from humble 'schools of literacy' to 'People's' or 'Free' (i.e. not State-controlled)

universities. It was a time described by one American authority on Russian education, with special reference to the ten years preceding the First World War, as 'a period [in Russia] of internal progress highlighted by a phenomenal expansion of educational opportunity'.

The tension, the urgency and the need for experimentation and for 'a phenomenal expansion of educational opportunity' can be readily understood when it is remembered that at the time of Nicholas II's accession to the throne Russia was, to all intents and purposes, a nation of illiterates: not much more than a quarter of its inhabitants of the age of ten and over could either read or write. The precise figure given by the 1897 Census is 27.8 per cent, an abysmally low proportion, even though the comparison with Western Europe, so inevitably made, is not entirely valid since the Russian statistics include the colonial and semi-colonial minorities in the Caucasus, Siberia, and Central Asia.

However, hardly less impressive than the extent of illiteracy at the beginning of the reign was the success of the fight against illiteracy at the end of it: in twenty years the proportion of the population able to read and write jumped from just over a quarter to nearly half. In other words, taking the population expansion into account, about twice as many persons were literate in 1917 as there had been two decades previously. The authorities could look forward with a fair measure of confidence to wiping out illiteracy altogether or, at least, reducing it to negligible proportions, except among the very old, by the middle or end of the 1920s: the law introducing primary education for all children of 8–11 inclusive was passed in 1908* and was applied so energetically that by 1915 more than half of all the children of relevant age were receiving primary education.

In that year, in spite of all the difficulties caused by the war and the internal unrest, a bill was introduced in the Duma (Russia's House of Commons) to make primary education compulsory and universal. The Ministry of Education also started work on a new plan to introduce compulsory secondary education by 1925, raising the

* This did not affect Finland and the Baltic Provinces within the Russian Empire, where schooling had been universal since the nineteenth century.

school leaving age to fifteen and thus placing Russia among the educationally more advanced countries. The plan hinged on the creation of a unified system of education in place of the existing complicated tangle of educational establishments controlled by numerous Departments of State, local government authorities, the Church, charitable foundations, and private organizations. Additional to these were the many schools organized and financed by orphanages and by factories for the children of their workers, as well as schools of the various national and religious minorities Christian and non-Christian, such as the Jewish *kheder* and the Muslim *mektebe*, important in a country which included about seven million Jews and 20–25 million Muslims among its inhabitants.

The drive to increase the number and size of primary schools on the whole succeeded admirably: by 1915 there were over twice as many primary schools and three times as many pupils as there were at the beginning of the reign. However, the quality of the teaching was generally low. Most primary schools, particularly in the villages, had a single teacher who sometimes, but by no means always, had an assistant. The children were taught little more than the three Rs and 'Divinity' (Catechism and Bible stories), but they could, at the age of ten, be transferred to a Higher Primary School, where during three or four years they were subjected to a terrifyingly full course of studies.

Perhaps the most interesting development in primary education was the rapid growth of 'schools of literacy'. These provided a very elementary form of education – little beyond reading and writing – usually free of charge, but sometimes charging the equivalent of a penny or two a month. The driving force behind them was the enthusiasm of private individuals who started them and who did all the teaching themselves. Often they were started on the initiative of peasants living in remote villages to which access was difficult because of lack of communications and, after 1905, also because of the general unrest and revolutionary activity. Though the schools were naturally intended for children, the pupils were quite often grown-up men and women. The success of these schools, particularly in the Asiatic provinces, was immense. In Siberia their number

was five or six times greater than that of official schools. All over Russia many a village which could boast of one official school, had two or three 'schools of literacy' as well.

Secondary education was, like primary, shared by a number of ministries, institutions, local authorities, and private establishments. The typical school, known as *gimnaziya* – grammar school may be an adequate translation – accepted children at the age of ten and kept them till they were seventeen. Parallel to the boys' *gimnazii* were the so-called '*realnyie*' colleges (a translation of the German '*Realschule*'), corresponding in some ways to the British Secondary Modern schools. Latin (and sometimes Greek), obligatory in the *gimnazii*, were not taught in them, but the curriculum in the upper forms included such subjects as book-keeping and principles of commerce. These latter subjects were at first given even greater emphasis in still another type of school known as Commercial. But Commercial schools gradually became almost identical to the *realnyie*, retaining their name for a technical but important reason: the principle of a percentage quota for Jewish children, applied in the boys' (though not the girls') *gimnazii* and in '*realnyie*' colleges prior to 1915, was not applicable to the Commercial schools (except for a short and fairly exceptional time). There were, too, a number of naval and military colleges ('Cadet Corps') as well as vocational, technical, and craft schools which included a programme of general education. A new type of school was started in 1907 and had great success: the so-called People's School, which provided evening classes for adult men and women for an insignificant fee.

The network of secondary schools was expanding throughout the reign with quite astonishing rapidity, the number of pupils doubling every ten years. Even so, it remained an inadequate network, concentrated mainly in urban areas. However, this did not seem to deter peasant children from increasingly attending these schools, more so, in fact, than the children of other social groups. So that if in the first year of Nicholas II's reign less than 10 per cent of all pupils in Government Secondary Schools (*gimnazii* and *Realschulen*) were children of peasants, twenty years later they represented as much as about a third of the total.

A group of young teachers.

A few schools remained bastions of privilege to the very end, but for that very reason involved an insignificant number of children. Socially the most ambitious of the boys' schools were His Imperial Majesty's Corps of Pages, the Emperor Alexander Lyceum and the Imperial Law College. All three were mainly for boarders and gave a complete education for boys from about the age of ten up to and including University level in the so-called 'special' forms, which ranked as Higher Education Establishments. The Corps of Pages was a military school reserved for sons of the more important gentry families and of high-ranking officers and officials. All the boys were referred to

as 'Pages' and some of the senior ones as 'Pages to the Imperial Household' (*Kamerpazhy*), thus emphasizing their special relationship to the Court. All of them wore military-type uniforms, resplendent on festive occasions, and the *Kamerpazhy* were detailed to attend the Emperor and Empress and other members of the Imperial family at certain ceremonial and public functions. After graduation most of them received their commission and were expected to serve at least three years, preferably in the Guards if their pass marks were sufficiently high. For a time after the Revolution the school was closed, as was to be expected. But strangely enough, it was reopened again in

Stalin's day, under new management and another name, but still in the same magnificent eighteenth-century mansion in Leningrad (Vorontsov House) and made once more into an élite military school, which it still is. It has been renamed Suvorov College after Imperial Russia's greatest soldier, as if to mark its historical continuity and its pre-eminence among military schools.

The Alexander Lyceum, whose main title to glory was that Pushkin was its pupil in the nineteenth century, provided a general education for sons of the gentry, while the Imperial Law College was, as its name implied, oriented towards legal studies. It was empowered to grant degrees to graduates of its 'special' forms, who were expected, after graduation, to work for a few years as civil servants in the Ministry of Justice.

The girls had their boarding schools too, known as Institutes. Though not as exclusive as the three boys' colleges just mentioned, they were, with a few exceptions, restricted (at least in theory) to the gentry and the urban middle classes. In spirit and intention these were probably near enough to the English public schools, except that the upper forms were equivalent to a university. The most famous of these Institutes was the Smolny 'for girls of gentle birth', founded by Catherine the Great. Nowadays it owes its fame – and its attraction for tourists and Communist pilgrims – to the fact that the palatial building (on the banks of the Neva) was occupied by the first Petrograd Soviet during the Revolution and became Lenin's H.Q. It is now occupied by various Communist Party offices.

On the eve of the 1917 Revolution the privileged schools, whether for boys or for girls, were no more than survivals from the past, about to be modified out of all recognition or simply abolished outright. The Russian educational system was being transformed to suit the more modern concepts and conditions imposed by social change and economic and technical necessity.

There was one feature of Russian school life that sounds familiar to present-day Western ears, however outlandish it might have appeared to them then: the participation of school children in strikes and political protests. Russian youth, it must be admitted, was in this respect well in advance of Western standards. As early as 1903 the Ministry of the Interior was complaining that in

at least one city the children had organized 'a fighting branch' to conduct 'active opposition to the detestable school regime'. As the 1905 revolutionary movement gathered momentum, children in many schools went on strike, organized demonstrations, suffered casualties as a result of police action, but were able to force the Government to adopt certain school reforms.

Universities. On the eve of the Revolution the Empire possessed about 90 Higher Education Establishments with about 125,000 students – 90,000 men and 30,000 women. Included in these H.E.E.s were twelve State Universities mostly founded in the nineteenth century, though some were more ancient.* Ten new universities were proposed by the Ministry of Education in 1915, but of these there was time and resources to found only one (Perm) before the crash came two years later. For historical and largely fortuitous reasons Russian universities – all of them State institutions – were reserved entirely for the study of 'pure' science (including history, jurisprudence, philosophy, and philology). They had no Faculty of Theology (except in Dorpat) or applied sciences (agriculture, mining etc.) and therefore those wishing to study these things went to Theological Academies (of which there were four), Mining Institutes, Agricultural Colleges and so forth, which had the status approximating to the French *Grandes Écoles*. Besides, a number of secondary schools, as already described, had 'special' forms where subjects were taught and lectures given on a university level. Since the entry of women into universities was restricted after the 1860s until allowed again in 1915, women's colleges were created (some twenty-five of them) which were not officially granted the name of 'university' though in fact enjoying equivalent status and standards.

Socially, the difference between the Russian and the British (or, rather, English) universities at the time was very striking. 'The great families of Russia', reported the delegation sent by the British Board of Education to investigate the Russian

* The 12 universities were Moscow, Kiev ('St Vladimir'), Kazan, Dorpat, Kharkov, St Petersburg, Odessa, Tomsk, Saratov, Perm, Rostov-on-Don and Helsingfors (now Helsinki). The university in Rostov-on-Don was the Warsaw University transferred to Rostov as an emergency measure for the duration of the war.

educational system in 1909, 'do not as a rule send their sons to universities, preferring to have them educated at select aristocratic schools such as the Alexander Lyceum, the School of Law or the Corps des Pages. The universities have, therefore, never had any such share in the training of the ruling classes as has fallen to the lot of Oxford and Cambridge.' Indeed, towards the end of the Imperial regime, Higher Education Establishments in Russia were transforming themselves with increasing rapidity from predominantly middle class to predominantly working class institutions, the number of students with a peasant background growing particularly fast. Thus, in 1880 urban workers and craftsmen in State universities accounted for only 12.4 per cent of the total student body and peasants for another 3.3 per cent – a total of just under 16 per cent. By 1914 their respective shares were 24.3 per cent and 14.5 per cent respectively – almost two-fifths of all students. In H.E.E.s other than State universities they accounted for well over half the total number of undergraduates. They came, on the whole, from poor and very poor families, with the result that the overwhelming majority of Russian undergraduates were not only freed from payment of any fees (which in any case were extremely low), but were dependent on Government grants and on bursaries founded by societies and private individuals.

But the relationship between students and Government was hardly a happy one. Protests and demonstrations were the order of the day, with students objecting not only to the Government's treatment of H.E.E.s – excessive interference with programmes, police surveillance, insufficient autonomy – but to Government policy as a whole, foreign and domestic. As so often in Russia, both protest and retaliation took extreme forms: no less than three ministers of the Crown were murdered by students in 1900–1904, while the Government had recourse to mass (if only temporary) expulsions, which served to exasperate feelings still further. The Russian nineteenth-century educationalist Pirogov once referred to undergraduates as 'the barometer of society'. It was an apt description: the barometer was pointing to 'Stormy'.

An interesting development, which began in the first years of Nicholas II's reign, was the establishment of 'People's' or 'Free' (i.e. non-State) universities outside the system of official H.E.E.s — colleges under Municipal control, of which by 1917 there were some twenty to thirty, spread all over the country from the Baltic Provinces to Central Asia. The most famous, though by no means the largest, of these was the Shanyavsky University in Moscow, which by 1914 had nearly 6,000 mainly part-time students, half of whom were women. When, as a protest against the restriction by the Government of the Moscow State University's autonomous status in 1911, the academic staff of the M.S.U. resigned *en bloc*, the Shanyavsky University opened its doors to them and thereby enhanced its own reputation and the quality of its teaching. Though not empowered to confer degrees, it could issue diplomas which were highly regarded.

To 'People's Universities' of the Shanyavsky type were added 'Peasant Universities' founded on the Scandinavian model in the years immediately preceding the First World War. It was an imaginative experiment, but the absence of State control which it implied failed to appeal to the Communist Government, and all 'Free' universities, whether 'People's' or 'Peasant', were closed almost immediately after Lenin's seizure of power. All voluntary secondary schools and institutes of adult education suffered the same fate.

It is interesting to note that while the attitude of contemporary Russians to their educational system, and particularly to the part played in it by the Government, was highly critical, foreigners were on the whole more favourably impressed. Such a long-standing observer of Russia as Maurice Baring, writing in 1914, only a few years before the Revolution, found 'the average Russian of the educated middle class . . . extremely well educated – so much better educated than the average educated Englishman that comparison would be silly'. And in the eyes of an American educational expert examining the Tsarist scene over fifty years later, 'the evidence remains impressive . . . that whatever its failings in other areas . . . in general education tsardom was working hard, productively, and intelligently at the moment when military disaster retired it from history'.

The main effort of the government was directed, of course, towards the *extension* of education to and among all classes of the population. That the *standard* of education was fairly high – however limited its extension – is surely suggested by at least this: that in the cultural sphere, the sphere of artistic experiment and achievement, Russia was able, for a brief moment before being overwhelmed by its revolution, to assume a place in the front rank, perhaps even take over the leadership, of the European world. That brief moment began, as so much else seems to have done in Russia, in the 1890s.

T he twentieth-century Russian theatre was born at 8 a.m. on 22 June 1897.* At two o'clock in the afternoon of the previous day two men met in a Moscow restaurant for a business chat. They left it late that night and, still talking, drove to the railway station, took the train to a town twenty-five miles away, continued their journey by cab and finally reached the country house of one of them. The conversation flowed on without a break in train, cab and house, till, finally, at eight o'clock the following morning, they rose from their armchairs, satisfied that the purpose of their meeting and of their eighteen-hour long discussion had been achieved: the idea of the Moscow Art Theatre, worked out in surprising detail, was ready to be launched.

The two contestants – it really seems the right word – were Nemirovich-Danchenko and Stanislavsky, who were to become world-famous both for their theatre and as producers. Nemirovich-Danchenko was later to claim (only half in jest) that the M.A.T.'s success was due in great measure to yet a third person, apart from Stanislavsky and himself: a Gypsy fortune-teller whom he consulted about the most propitious date for the opening. Her advice was, it is true, a little vague. Nemirovich, she said, was to take 'some sort of middle figure', which, apparently, excluded the fifth, tenth, and fifteenth of any month, and a day of 'no particular account', i.e. not Saturday, Sunday, or Monday. Wednesday, 14 October 1898 seemed to satisfy these requirements and that date was accordingly chosen.

The M.A.T. marked a turning point in the Russian theatre, away from classical traditions towards greater realism, freedom of interpretation

* Eastern calendar. In Western Europe the date was 4 July.

and attention to detail. It laid stress on team work rather than on individual 'stars' and thus enhanced the role of the producer at the expense, it is often said, of the actor. Henceforth it was producers that dominated the Russian theatre – Stanislavsky and Nemirovich-Danchenko in Moscow, Komissarzhevskaya and Meyerhold in St Petersburg are probably the most familiar names. It was a theatre of experimentation. But the experiments were eventually to lead the Russian theatre away from Stanislavsky's and the M.A.T.'s realism to Vakhtangov's Synthesism (mixture of realism and artifice), Meyerhold's Expressionism, Tairov's Rhythmic Unity (blend of music, drama, gesture, and decor in which each of these elements fulfilled equally important roles), and finally to 'trans-sense' Futurism of plays in which actors, dressed in cardboard held together by wire, wore masks looking like modern gas-masks, and sang songs consisting either entirely of consonants or entirely of vowels. Plays, such as this 1913 production, continued right through the war. Kruchyonykh's 'Gli-gli', a mixture of noises, bright colours, lighting effects, 'trans-sense' language, dancing, mime, acting, and clowning resulted in fights between the actors and the totally bewildered audience. 'Gli-gli' was running (or perhaps more exactly, fighting its way) on a Moscow coffee bar stage when the October Revolution overwhelmed the country and put a stop a few years later to theatre experimentation.

But until that happened, experiments went on and, surprisingly, were not limited to the private stage, but were allowed scope in the Imperial (i.e. State) theatres too, as, for instance, in the Alexandra Theatre in St Petersburg under Meyerhold's direction. On the whole, however, Imperial theatres were more traditional and staid than the ever-growing number of private enterprises. And they never did set out, as the M.A.T. deliberately did, to be 'literary'. By that the M.A.T.'s founders meant that they would endeavour to promote the interests of Russian literature by helping contemporary authors to produce their works on the stage. Chekhov, Gorki, Leonid Andreyev all benefited by that policy and are evidence of its success.

It is typical of the age and of the country that when the organisers of the M.A.T. published the programme of principles which were to regulate their new venture, they should have put at the head of it the democratization of the audience: the first aim of their policy, they said, must be 'to enable the poor classes and especially the indigent intelligentsia to have good seats in the theatre at a low price'. The same aim, in fact, was being pursued by the Government at about the same time. In furtherance of it, the so-called People's Palace was opened in St Petersburg at the beginning of the century on the initiative and with the active encouragement of Nicholas II. A rash of these People's Palaces sprang up all over Russia — for the most part municipal, others founded on private initiative and financed by private individuals. Their main feature was always a theatre, a concert hall and an opera house, with seats if not free, at least very nearly so, as well as a non-paying choir-school, a free library, and a number of lecture halls. For those whose brow was regrettably low, there was always an amusements arcade. Of the two People's Palaces in St Petersburg, 'Nicholas II's' and the 'Ligovsky' (financed by Countess Panin), the former was the larger. It combined a theatre (which was a separate building, seating three thousand spectators) with a concert and an opera house, where standing room cost one penny in present-day English money, and the most expensive seat in the Stalls cost the equivalent of ten to fifteen new pence. The level of performance was the highest available, since all the best Russian and foreign visiting companies and artists (Chaliapine, Batistini, Tetrazzini etc.) could be heard there. It was an immensely popular institution, drawing, in the words of *The Times* correspondent, 'crowds of working people, artisans and soldiers who are given the opportunity of becoming acquainted with a great variety of standard operas, both Russian and foreign'. The former included, of course, not only the nineteenth-century operas of Glinka and Tchaikovsky, but also the early twentieth-century ones of Rimsky-Korsakov and others. Stravinsky's operas (very few in any case) came much later and were all (except for 'The Nightingale') composed after the Revolution when he was living abroad as a refugee.

Opera was a great favourite with the Russians, with the result that St Petersburg alone had four opera houses, including the People's Palaces.

Moscow and the larger provincial cities such as Kiev, Odessa and Tiflis also had opera houses with permanent companies giving performances during seasons which lasted eight to nine months in the year. Especially popular was the Italian opera, but since the Italian companies concentrated entirely on the voices of singers, the quality of their operatic production suffered considerably; acting they regarded as quite superfluous. Masini, one of the world's greatest tenors at the time, never even gave it a thought. At one of his performances in St Petersburg, when the stage 'business' required the soprano to sing a long lament over the body of the dying tenor, Masini, bored by having to lie still, suddenly got up and walked away. The soprano went on operatically crying her heart out over the empty floor-boards till the moment came for Masini to sing again. He then came back, perfectly unconcerned, and lay down on the spot where he had been lying before.

It was in protest against performances such as this that the Musical Drama Theatre in St Petersburg set out to reform operatic productions by abolishing most, if not all, operatic conventions, and that Chaliapine decided to become — and became — as great an actor as he was a singer.

Russian music at the time was passing, like all the arts in Russia, through a revolutionary stage. Scriabin, Stravinsky and the very young Prokofiev spring to mind, though the more traditional elements were well represented by such composers as Glazunov, Lyadov, Rachmaninov, and the last survivors of Russian nineteenth-century musical nationalism — Balakirev and Rimsky-Korsakov. Scriabin was in many ways one of the most revolutionary of all Russian composers at the time. His early works date back to the 1890s and he continued to compose right up to his death in 1915. Theosophy and mysticism played a large part in his life, and under their influence he developed a harmonic style or system — including his 'mystic chord' — which was meant to give expression to these ideas. His 'use of the mystic chord', says a modern historian of Russian music, 'inevitably invites comparison with the twelve-note method of composition to which Schoenberg was to come some years later', even if the validity of the comparison can be (and is) disputed. Scriabin believed in the synthesis of all the arts, but he gave this synthesis a kind of

A Carnival-time cabaret at the Moscow Art Theatre, 1910. Founded in 1894, the theatre had made an astonishing impact by its ensemble acting, most notably in Chekhov's plays. Both founders of the theatre, Stanislavsky and Nemirovich-Danchenko, are present: Stanislavsky – centre right, white hair, hand to cheek; Nemirovich-Danchenko – centre, bearded and above the smiling lady in white.

eschatological significance. He referred to it as 'the Mystery', for it was to lead, in a way known only to the initiated, to the regeneration of the world. The contemporary critics found his later compositions 'unfamiliar and dissonant' and he had to wait till our own day to be suddenly taken up in the West (especially by the young) and have the coda of his 'Poem of Ecstasy' described approvingly as 'a species of psychedelic exaltation'. But the more orthodox modern tendency is to regard Scriabin as 'an expendable curiosity'.

Stravinsky, a much more significant figure, was not impressed by what he describes as Scriabin's 'ideological verbosities'. He was not himself mystically inclined and, in any case, refused to regard music as a reflection of anything beyond itself. 'I hold music', he said, 'to be essentially powerless to express anything whatsoever, be it a feeling, an attitude, a state of mind or a natural phenomenon . . . If music seems to express something, this is merely an illusion'. Of all Russian composers active during the reign of the last Russian sovereign, Stravinsky is probably universally the best known ('the Picasso of music' is by now a well-worn phrase). In the West his name first became familiar through his association with Diaghilev, when, a few years before World War I, the 'Ballets-Russes' came to Paris and performed *The Firebird*, *Petrushka* and *The Rite of Spring* for which Stravinsky had composed the music.

The 'Ballets-Russes' were by no means the same as the (Imperial) Russian Ballet, even though the same dancers performed in both. The first was a private enterprise, the second an official institution attached to the Court and financed out of the Emperor's Privy Purse. Nowadays it is ballet – the Imperial Ballet – that is usually regarded in the West as the quintessence of all that Imperial Russia stood for artistically. At that time, however, in the West the ballet as such was hardly considered to be an art-form at all. To the *Encyclopaedia Britannica* (1910 edition) it was morally suspect ('a spectacle, the chief interest of which is quite independent of dancing') and, in any case, a sheer waste of money. 'Thousands of pounds,' it lamented, 'are spent on dressing a small army of women, who do little but march about the stage and group themselves in accordance with some design of colour and mass; no

more is asked of the intelligence than to believe that a ballet dressed, for example, in military uniform is a compliment to or glorification of the army.' Besides, it had no future, for 'it seems unlikely that we shall see any revival of the best period and styles of dancing until a higher standard of grace and manners becomes fashionable in society' – an improbable occurrence. This was published at the time when in far-off Russia, which was not even worth a mention, Kshessinskaya, Pavlova, Karsavina, Nijinsky were all appearing on the Maryinsky stage in St Petersburg, when Fokine was both dancer and choreographer, Bakst, Korovin, and Golovin were stage designers, and Diaghilev's 'Ballets-Russes' had just made an artistic conquest of Paris. In fact, Diaghilev's 'Ballets-Russes' (by their performances in France) and the Russian Revolution (by forcing these dancers out of Russia) have since combined to make them household names in the Western world.

Unlike ballet in Paris or London, the Imperial ballet did not serve as a mere *divertissement*, thrown in to enliven theatrical or operatic performances. Its performances were quite independent and based on long libretti lasting a whole evening. Wednesdays and Sundays in the Maryinsky (now Kirov) Theatre were ballet nights. Balletomanes – venerable civil servants and army generals – armed with binoculars, occupied the best seats in the Stalls, and analysed, criticized, praised, and blamed the performance of each dancer. The boxes – other than the Royal, the Grand-Ducal, and the Director's – were for the most part occupied by subscribers: either private families or clubs such as the grand and exclusive Yacht Club or English Club or regiments like the Horse Guards. A private individual would have found it difficult, if not impossible, to book a box for the season. The ballet had become a social institution.

This, in fact, was just its trouble, for it inevitably became conventionalized and to some extent stereotyped, the scene sets, though opulent and often attractive, were equally often heavy, pompous, and lacking in variety, and the treatment of music was unimaginative. Reform began in the early years of this century, and it was the great contribution of Fokine to be one of the first to instil a sense of drama into ballet, to give characterization to the roles of dancers, even those in the *corps de ballet*, and to demand of them some understanding of the music to which they danced. As time went on, Fokine, strongly influenced by Diaghilev, increasingly stressed the role and importance of music in ballet and insisted that it was not to be treated as a mere accompaniment to the dance; it was 'an organic part' of it, and its quality, he said, determined the quality of the choreography.

Fokine's reformist zeal made him gravitate to a group of men who, viewing art as one indivisible whole, revolutionized it in all its aspects and started a new artistic era in Russia. It was the group responsible for the movement known as the 'World of Art'. It has been compared to the *Art Nouveau* movement in Western Europe, and, like it, it represented the artistic *avant-garde* of the time. But it was more all-embracing, and involved painting, literature, music, theatre, ballet – 'the whole of life', in fact, according to Alexander Benois (1870–1960), one of its founders. Benois's own many-sidedness matched the claims he made on behalf of his movement: 'Painter, theatrical designer, producer, scholar, art critic, art historian, Benois', says Camilla Gray, 'is the epitome of what the World of Art came to stand for'. And by a stroke of extraordinary luck, he found a collaborator who, without being proficient in any of the arts, had a creative appreciation of all of them and a genius for inspiring artists to give of their best. To this he joined a formidable organizing ability and a gift for inducing enthusiastic co-operation among the least co-operative of people. His name was Diaghilev.

Diaghilev became the editor of the 'World of Art' magazine, whose first number appeared in 1898, and an energetic promoter of Russian art in general, and particularly, at that time, of Russian painting and painters. Russian painting was, just then, turning an important corner – away from utilitarianism, which regarded art as a pulpit from which to preach, to censure and to praise moral behaviour and civic virtues. Vrubel's was the initiating influence, in the direction towards art as an independent activity, governed by its own laws and serving its own goals – 'Art for Art's sake', in short. Yet Vrubel himself was greatly influenced by the Symbolist movement which few countries escaped in the 1890s. This,

along with his failure to assimilate the lessons of French impressionism has assured his neglect, for all his historical importance, by present-day artists. In 1905 he seems to have struck out on a new path in his portrait of the poet Bryusov. It was probably the first Russian work in which Cubism played an original and constructive part. Moreover, the way in which Vrubel used this new technique was to become typical of Russian Cubism thereafter: the geometric design aimed, as Tamara Talbot Rice suggests in discussing Russian Cubo-Futurism, at attaining the essence of the object represented (animate or inanimate), and not, as used by most Western artists, merely to obtain a three-dimensional effect.

The link between Vrubel and the 'World of Art' was to a considerable extent provided by Valentin Serov (the composer's son), perhaps the most sensitive of Russian portraitists, though very much a traditionalist in outlook and technique. Other 'World of Art' painters, like Somov, Lanceray, Röhrich, were of lesser significance, though of some importance for the evolution of Russian pictorial art. None of them thought of himself as internationally important. Except Bakst. 'I am,' he used to say with genuine conviction, 'certainly the greatest painter in the world,' adding for good measure: 'I am the Russian Velasquez.' But no-one took him literally and he continued to be appreciated mainly (he would have said, merely) as a gifted creator of stage sets, back-cloths and costumes. Nevertheless, however local the significance of many 'World of Art' artists, they were able to arouse such an interest in painting that collecting became a dominant passion among those who could afford it, mainly among rich Moscow business tycoons. The personal taste of these men drove them to buy not only products of Russian art, but also, and sometimes exclusively, French paintings of the latest schools. The result was that Moscow could now boast of vast collections of French impressionists and post-impressionists, of cubists and *fauvistes*, of Cézanne, Monet, Gauguin, as well as of Matisse, Braque, and Picasso. Besides, the quality of these collections was such that artistically 'the most advanced ideas and movements . . . were even more familiar in Moscow than in Paris itself'.

These could not but influence Russian artists and help them to break away, in their turn, from

The dining-room in the eighteenth-century Trubetskoy Palace,
the Moscow mansion of Sergey Shchukin, one of six brothers, all collectors.
He formed perhaps the greatest collection of modern French art at the time.
The large painting in the centre of the right-hand wall is Monet's sketch
for Le Déjeuner sur l'herbe. *An adjacent salon contained more than twenty Matisses.*
It is interesting to note that Shchukin's taste
extended to the Burne-Jones tapestry on the back wall.

the 'World of Art' movement. They helped them, too, to evolve their own schools of painting, and by the end of the first decade of the present century Russian artists were able to free themselves from too much West European influence and not only establish their own independent styles, but become 'pioneers in the "modern movement"'. From a provincial backwater, Russia emerged, with dramatic suddenness, as 'a truly international centre', 'a meeting place for the most revolutionary ideas in European art'. Russia had become the stage for what Camilla Gray has called 'the Great Experiment'.

Ideas and movements proliferated: Primitivism, Rayonnism, Cubo-futurism, Constructivism, Suprematism associated with the names of Larionov and Goncharova, the Burliuk brothers and Alexandra Exter, Tatlin and Malevich and a host of others; Surrealism, of which Chagall, then still a Russian painter (he became French after the Revolution), was the first and – according to some – the only true exponent, since it was to his work, while he was on a visit to Paris just before World War I, that Guillaume Apollinaire first applied that description.

Clearly, the Russian artists were not only influencing artists in the West – they were themselves influenced by them. But the Western influence was often re-interpreted in a way which made the Russian product into an original contribution, as was the case of Cubism. The same was true of Cubo-Futurism – of all new artistic movements the one most widely adopted in Russia. They were keen to co-operate with movements and schools abroad, and did – with such as the *Blaue Reiter*, which Kandinsky, Yavlensky and a number of other Russian artists helped to create in Munich. The experiments were endless, and they spilled out into the early post-revolutionary years, finally petering out under pressure of official disapproval in the 1920s.

The experiments, however, were not always carried out in a spirit of perfect amity. Malevich's Suprematism – coloured geometric patterns, consisting of circles, rectangles, crosses and triangles – aroused furious opposition among other *avant-garde* artists. So much so that at an exhibition in Petrograd – ex-St Petersburg – in December 1915 (called typically for the period, '0.10. The Last Futurist Painting Exhibition'), Malevich and the Constructivist Tatlin came to blows. They were separated before Malevich (much the taller and the stronger of the two) could knock out his opponent, but he nevertheless defeated him in the popularity stakes. Suprematist painting became all the rage in Moscow, even among people not ordinarily interested in art. *Succès de scandale* no doubt, but it is curious to note that with the war in full swing, the collapse of the Imperial regime only a few weeks away and the Liberal Party leader Miliukov pointing out that the fate of the country was in the balance, some Moscow newspapers were able to report: 'People are almost equally interested in Suprematist painting, *Pamira Kifared* [an *avant-garde* play produced by Tairov, with Futurist sets and scenery] and the speeches of Miliukov in the Duma'.

All these developments in painting and the theatre, as well as in music, were, of course, closely paralleled by developments in Russian literature. The revolt against realism – against didactic realism, to begin with – can also be traced back to the 1890s when two currents of thought, different in expression, but psychologically linked, diverted the Russian intelligentsia from its exclusive concentration on social and political problems. One was its newly-found interest in religion (in place of the hitherto obligatory atheism or, at least, agnosticism) and the other – the modernist movement i.e. literature in which aestheticism and mysticism played a predominant part. The first reinvigorated Russian philosophy – what there was of it – and helped to lift the Russian Church out of its mental torpor by the re-interpretation of its dogmas. In much of this, men like Berdyaev, Bulgakov, Frank and the Trubetskoy brothers continued and developed the work of their predecessors such as Khomyakov and Solovyov. The second, through its main offshoot, Symbolism, 'substituted beauty for duty', in D. S. Mirsky's suggestive phrase. Symbolism, largely through French influence via the innovations of Valériy Bryusov and, to some extent, of Balmont, gave a new impetus to Russian poetry which, by the 1890s, had become drained of all vitality and was reduced largely to versification, either lachrymose or trite or both, much of it on 'civic' themes. For Symbolist writers e.g. Bryusov, Bely, Blok, Vyacheslav Ivanov, Zinaida Hippius, were first and foremost poets, even when they wrote in prose, even when, like Remizov, they wrote only in prose. And by influencing almost all subsequent literary movements they earned for the twenty-five years preceding the Revolution the name of the Silver Age of Russian poetry, or even of the Second Golden Age, the First being that of Pushkin three or four generations earlier.

However, the older Russian literary tradition was not taken over entirely by the new movement; it had not simply ceased to exist. Tolstoy, after all, was still very much alive and a force to be reckoned with throughout most of this period; Chekhov was at his best during the first half of it; Gorki, looked up to (mistakenly) as Tolstoy's heir, was entirely its product and his value as a writer hardly survived it for more than a very few years even though he continued to write till his death in 1936. Probably the most significant traditionalist writer of the epoch was Bunin. Not as romantic as Gorki, he had a more sensitive ear for language and a greater capacity for individualization of character. He did deal with the social scene, but was careful not to preach or convey a sense of social outrage. That alone would have distinguished him from the old-fashioned radical intelligentsia. The fact that he was not only a prose writer, but also a poet with a strong religious sense, emphasized this distinction and provided a link between him and the Symbolists with whom he had otherwise nothing in common.

Most Symbolists tended to regard any art, including literature, as an essentially religious activity, aesthetics being no more than its formal aspect. Indeed, to Bely, the most articulate of Symbolist theoreticians, 'art has no meaning of its own apart from a religious one'. Unable to accept this mystic approach, an important group of poets, headed by Gumilyov, hived off from the Symbolists and founded another school to which they gave the name of Acmeism. *Akme* is Greek for 'point' or 'sharp edge': the Acmeists aimed at achieving in their language clarity, precision and hardness of outline, while retaining the symbolic, though not the religious, aspect of Symbolism. Curiously enough, many thousands of miles away, Ezra Pound and T. S. Eliot were attempting precisely this at precisely the same time, and calling it Imagism. The names of some of the Acmeists have recently (though posthumously)

become familiar in the West, among them Mandelstam and Anna Akhmatova, for reasons, however, which probably have more to do with politics than literature.

The proliferation of literary tendencies and schools let loose by Symbolism was truly impressive. All of them shared with the Symbolists the desire to break down clichés and to free words and images from the connotations and associations with which they had become encrusted. This is true of the 'Peasant Poets' — Klyuev and Esenin — of Marina Tsvetayeva, who is largely outside all 'movements', and above all of the Futurists who went much further than anyone else. A moderate Futurist like Pasternak was able to enliven and enrich the language and convey a feeling of freshness and originality through unexpected similes and a use of words which was sometimes idiosyncratic, but perfectly understandable. (Pasternak began publishing his works before World War I, but the most important of all his collections of poems (*My Sister Life*) appeared in 1917 — the year of the Revolution — and can thus just be included in our period.) The more extreme Futurists, however, such as Kruchyonykh, resorted to a wholesale coining of new words and to the use of a language which they called 'transsense', which sometimes limited itself to nothing but a series of consonants or vowels, but which they hoped would develop into a world language.

The first Futurist poem, which appeared in 1910 and was written by Khlebnikov, the founder of the movement, consisted essentially of one word only: *Smekh*, Russian for 'laughter', to which was appended a great number of its derivatives invented by the author. Nevertheless, Khlebnikov had an acute ear for the 'genius' and sound of language; his inventions *sounded* Russian and, therefore, many of them took root and influenced later writers. He certainly never showed much keenness to influence his listeners. At public poetry readings, always so popular in Russia, he would start declaiming a poem of his own, only to stop almost immediately and say: 'and so on and so forth'. The other Futurist innovation which did much to strengthen the language and give it freshness, was the attempt to disengage poetry from what is (or was) usually considered as 'poetic' or conventionally beautiful. 'We refuse,' the Futurists said in their inevitable Manifesto, 'to see any distinction between poetry, prose and everyday speech.' Mayakovsky with his loud-mouthed verses, his cheerful crudeness, his punning rhymes, his earthiness, was perhaps the best exponent of this. He felt he had to show solidarity with his fellow Futurists in all forms of art and, accordingly, appeared with a group of Futurist painters walking about the streets of Moscow in cardboard clothes, his face painted with flowers and Suprematist designs. Together with David Burliuk whom he regarded as his teacher, he joined the 'Futurist Tour' which went all over Russia on a self-advertising spree. But Burliuk stole most of the limelight by wearing a notice on his forehead, which made people think he was the leader of the group. The notice said simply: 'I am Burliuk.'

Three years later, on the eve of the February revolution, a 'Carnival of the Arts' was held in Petrograd. A long line of flower-bedecked motor cars drove slowly down the main street. The cars were filled with artists; painters, composers, writers, and actors staring rather self-consciously at the crowd which watched them roll by. They were followed by a large lorry with the words: 'The Chairman of the Terrestrial Globe' chalked in big letters on its sides. The passenger sitting in the lorry was Khlebnikov.

When the October Revolution came the Futurists welcomed it with open arms and called themselves the 'Agents of the Social Order'. It was, they felt, *their* revolution, and Mayakovsky proclaimed himself its 'Drummer'. But the concept of Futurism as art for the masses was not shared by the masses, nor, for that matter, by the Communist Party or the Soviet Government, and instead of being, as it thought, the harbinger of the new age, the Futurist movement turned out to be an embarrassing legacy of the old. Burliuk was quick to sense this and quietly slipped away to the United States to become a well-known painter. Its founder, Khlebnikov, the former 'Chairman of the Terrestrial Globe', died of starvation and neglect in 1922, and eight years later Mayakovsky committed suicide. But by that time Futurism in Russia had ceased to exist.

However, it is only fair to add that its literary competitors fared no better. Blok and Gumilyov were the first to go, both of them in the late summer of 1921 – Blok dying of undernourishment, and Gumilyov put up against a wall in a prison yard and shot. Soon it was Esenin's turn to commit suicide, preceding Mayakovsky by a few years. Klyuev died in mysterious circumstances immediately after his temporary release from a concentration camp. Marina Tsvetayeva hanged herself soon after returning to Russia from the West where she had lived as a refugee, while Mandestam died of ill-treatment in a concentration camp. Pasternak's and Akhmatova's fate was less dramatic: they were merely forbidden to write or publish original work – at least for a time – and had to limit themselves to translation.

In the other arts, Kandinsky, Goncharova, Larionov, Chagall took refuge in Germany and France. Stravinsky, who happened to be in Switzerland at the time of the Revolution, simply never went back. Nor did Diaghilev, who was able to reconstitute his 'Ballets-Russes' outside Russia with the help of such survivors of the old team as Benois, Fokine, Karsavina, and others who succeeded in making their escape from the U.S.S.R.

'The Great Experiment' was over.

Notes

Page 12. An eight per cent rise in industrial production: Gerschenkron, 50–51 and 54.

12. 'revolutionary': Lenin, vol. 16, 424.

12. His own plans: *ibid.*, 407. 'to give up . . . society': Lenin, vol. 17, 275.

15. 'What am I going to do?': Alexander, 168. 'Lord, help us': Nicholas, 85. 'without fear'; 'the worst thing . . .': *ibid.*, 104.

15. 'We have been . . .': Alexandra, 464 (letter No. 401 of 14 Dec. 1916).

16. Three Abyssinians: Vorres, 26.

16. 'By a sudden . . .': Viroubova, 9.

17. Seldom saw anyone: Buxhoeveden, 158.

17. Some £2½m: Civil List c.17m.r. (varying), Khromov, 526–7. Imperial lands (*udely*) in 1896 (only year available to me) 5.2m.r., Brokgauz, vol. 34, SPb 1902 article: '*Udely*'. Interest on bank deposits £½m (implied by Alexander, 54, 55). Massie states 'total' income to be 24m.r. (£2.4m), but omits interest on bank deposits. Emperor's own share: Alexander, 183; Mossolov, 145. Empress's income: Almedingen, 56, gives 'just over £40,000' jointly with Nicholas, but Alexander, 56, gives £50,000. Emperor's and Empress's personal fortune: Benckendorff, 89. £/r. exchange rate assumed at £1 = 10 r.

18. Cordially disliked: Vorres, 100. Attempted assassination: Vorres, 120.

19. Hurried away: *ibid.*, 101. Fancy-dress ball: *ibid.*, 102.

19. Vote for a Republic: Nic. Mikh., 205. Letter dated '29 June/12 July 1917' (i.e. old/new style).

21. Officer corps of peasant origin: Garthoff, 326. Officer trainees: Luckett, 12.

23. 'for twenty-four friends . . .': Romanovsky, 163.

24. 'The house stands . . .': Williams, 363.

25. Owned or leased about 90 per cent: Chelintsev, 10.

25. Half the total 'Estate': Census, xiii.

30. Peasants' sown area and livestock: Chelintsev, 10–11; Lenin's attitude: Lenin, vol. XV, 246.

30. Kustari: Novy, vol. 23, column 756, article: '*Kustarnaya promyshlennost*'.

30. Number of industrial workers: Antoshkin, 14; Seton-Watson, 540; Zagorsky, 51; McCauley, 3.

32. Rooms warm and well ventilated: Palmer, 231–2; sombre picture: Pazhitnov, *passim*.

32–3. Izhevsk: Bork, 176.

33. Belgium: Finn, 380. Working hours: Antoshkin, 118. 1903 Act: Seton-Watson, 541. Trade Unions, Workers' compensation 1912; Antoshkin, 89. 'in its provisions . . .': Roosa, 452. Strikes: Finn, 367; Antoshkin, 199,200.

35. 'Merchants' in the Kremlin: Rabeneck.

35. '*Protsentshchik*': Buryshkin, 110.

36. Timofey Morozov and employees: Bill, 24. Korolyov: Buryshkin, 62, quoting Shchukin, P.I., *Kak v starinu pili moskovskiye kuptsy*.

36. 'Richesse oblige': Bowlt, 444.

36–7. Shchukin and Ivan Morozov: Ginsburg, 470–85.

37. Savva Morozov approached for funds for M.A.T.: Nemirovich, 110. Savva Morozov as architect of M.A.T.: Stanislavsky, 244–7. At no cost to the theatre: Sobolev, 74.

37. The Morozovs – Varvara, Michael, Ivan, Margarita: Ginsburg, 471–2.

37–8. Savva Morozov and Social-Democratic (Bolshevik) Party: Gorki.

38. Savva Morozov's suicide: Bill, 26. N. P. Schmidt: Schapiro, 109–10, 119, 130. Tikhomirnov preparing publication of *Pravda* 'at Lenin's behest': B.S.E., Tikhomirnovs as millionaire shipowners and founders of *Pravda*: Denike, 280–7.

41. Deacons: Alexeyev. Bank manager: Baring: 244.

43. Their own forks and spoons: Buryshkin, 119. *Khlysty*: Brokgauz, vol. 37, p. 406, article: *Khlysty*. Borovikovsky: Dubrovin, 230.

44. Half the Russian peasants as Old Ritualists and Sectarians: Aksakov, 90; Soloviev, 25. Old Ritualists and sectarians 20 and 25m: Milyukov, 155 and 157. On church reform see Zernov.

44. Seven million: Yevreyskoye, viii; Sliozberg, *Dorevolyutsionnyi*, 258, 276. Million and a quarter emigrants: Ettinger, 21. 'Queen of Jerusalem' and 'The Oath in the Temple': Cheshikhin, 517.

45. Jews as a third of Russia's trading community: Dijur, 126–43.

46. Percentage quota: Sliozberg, *Dela*, vol. I, 36; Greenberg, 33–6. 'apostate's garb': Sliozberg, *Dela*, vol. I, 71–2.

46. Artisans and petty traders: Dijur, 142. Seldom speaking anything but Yiddish and unable to read and write in Russian: Ettinger, 15; Brutskus, 35, 48. 'considered it sinful . . .': Deutsch, 17.

48. 200 different nationalities: 193 nationalities, according to the 1926 Population Census of the U.S.S.R. Over a quarter of that population: Matchenko, 72. 20–25m Muslims: Novy, vol. 27, column 577, article: '*Musulmanstvo*'. City of Kazan: Seton-Watson, 673; Zenkovsky, 121. Two million out of ten: *Aziatskaya*, vol. I, 86. Nine million Russian settlers: *ibid.*, 82. Stone-age culture: *ibid.*, 87.

50. 'something between a human dwelling and a beast's lair': *ibid.*, 192. Within six or seven years: *ibid.*, 196. Three million in seven years: *ibid.*, 81, 189.

53. 'a period of internal progress . . .': Alston, 200. From just over a quarter to nearly half: Timashev; Riasanovsky, 486. By 1915 more than half . . .: Anweiler, 306. Bill to make primary education compulsory: Hans, 219. Secondary education by 1925: Anweiler, 309. Raising school leaving age to 15: Kaidanova, Part I, 77.

54. Twice as many schools and three times as many pupils: Anweiler, 306; Hans, 233. Terrifyingly full course, Novy, vol. 28, p. 131 and 140, article: '*Nachalnoye narodnoye obrazovaniye*'. Two or three 'schools of literacy': Kaidanova, Part I, 95–6. Number of secondary school pupils doubling every ten years: Hans, 242. In the first year . . . the total: based on Hans, 233 and Alston, 289.

56. 'a fighting branch . . .': quoted by Alston, 167. On the eve . . . two years later: Hans, 206. 'The great families . . .': Darlington, 431.

57. In 1880 urban workers . . . students: Hans, 242. Dependence on grants and bursaries: Darlington, 431. 'barometer of society': quoted by Alston, 84. 20–30 People's Universities: Kaidanova, Part I, 367. Shanyavsky University, 6,000 students: *ibid.*, 370. Half of whom were women: Alston, 201. Moscow University staff joins Shanyavsky University: Kizevetter, 486. Diplomas granted by Shanyavsky University: *ibid.*, 492. 'the average Russian of the educated middle class . . .': Baring, 191. 'the evidence remains impressive . . .': Alston, 248.

58. At 2 o'clock in the afternoon . . . launched upon the world: Nemirovich, 64, 70, 72. Gipsy fortune-teller's advice: *ibid.*, 140. Gas masks and Futurist plays: Gray, 308. 'Gligli': *ibid.*, 197. Interests of Russian literature: Sobolev, 80.

59. 'To enable the poor classes . . .': *ibid.*, 80. People's Palaces: Novy, vol. 27, columns 948–9, article: 'Narodnye doma'. Description of 'Nicholas II' People's Palace: Williams,

266. 'crowds of working people . . .': *ibid.*, 266–7. Opera houses in St Petersburg, Moscow and the provinces: Florinsky, vol. II, 1251. Masini: Lieven, 69. 'use of the mystic chord . . .': Brown, 24.

61. 'A psychedelic exaltation': Robert Craft, quoted by Bowers, 112. 'an expendable curiosity': Brown, 26. 'ideological verbosities': Stravinsky (Calder and Boyars), 160. 'I hold music . . .': *ibid.*, 53, here quoted from Calvocoressi, 90. a spectacle the chief interest of which . . .': *Encyclopaedia Britannica*, 11th ed., vol. 3, London 1910, article: 'Ballet'.

62. 'an organic part': Karsavina, 169. 'Painter, theatrical designer . . .': Gray 35–6. essence of the object represented: Talbot Rice, 257. 'greatest painter . . . Velasquez': Lieven, 300–1.

64. 'pioneers . . .', '. . . international centre', 'a meeting place . . .': Gray, 65, 85, 86. Guillaume Apollinaire: Wilenski, 207, 231. 'People are almost equally . . .': Gray, 194.

65. 'and so on and so forth': Kamensky, 183. 'We refuse to see . . .': Slonim, 22.

66. Carnival of the arts: Kamensky, 211.

Bibliography

AKSAKOV, IVAN *Sochineniya*, vol. 4, Moscow, 1886

ALEXANDER MIKHAILOVICH, GRAND-DUKE *Once a Grand Duke*, Cassell, London, 1931

ALEXANDRA FEDOROVNA, EMPRESS *Letters to the Emperor Nicholas II*, Berlin, 1922

ALEXEYEV, V. 'Moskovskiye protodiakony' in *Novy Zhurnal*, nos 117 and 118, December 1974 and March 1975, New York

ALMEDINGEN, E. M. *The Empress Alexandra, 1872–1918*, Hutchinson, London, 1961

ALSTON, P. L. *Education and the State in Tsarist Russia*, Stamford University Press, 1969

ANTOSHKIN, D. *Professionalnoye dvizheniye v Rossii*, Moscow, 1924

ANWEILER, O. 'Russian Schools' in *Russia Enters the Twentieth Century 1894–1917*, Ed. E. Oberländer, G. Katkov, N. Poppe, G. v. Rauch, Methuen, London, 1973

Aziatskaya Rossiya, publ. by Pereselencheskoye upravleniye glavnavo upravleniya zemleustroystva i zemledeliya (Re-settlement Board), 2 vols, St Petersburg, 1914

BARING, MAURICE *The Mainsprings of Russia*, London, 1914

BENCKENDORFF, PAUL *Last Days at Tsarskoye Selo*, London 1935

BILL, V. T. *The Forgotten Class: The Russian Bourgeoisie from the Earliest Beginnings to 1900*, Praeger, New York, 1959

BORK, S. M. 'The "Class Tragedy" of Izhevsk: Working-class Opposition to Bolshevism in 1918' in *Russian History*, vol. 2, Part 2, University Center for University Studies, University of Pittsburg, 1975

BOWERS, FAUBION *The New Scriabin: Enigma and Answers*, David & Charles, Newton Abbott, 1974

BOWLT, JOHN 'Two Russian Maecenases: Savva Mamontov and Princess Tenisheva' in *Apollo*, December 1973, London

BROKGAUZ i EFRON *Entsiklopedicheskiy slovar*, St Petersburg, 1890–1904

BROWN, DAVID 'Russia' in *A History of Western Music*, vol. V: *Music in the Modern Age*. Ed. F. W. Sternfeld, Weidenfeld & Nicholson, London, 1973

BRUTSKUS, B. *Statistika yevreyskavo naseleniya*, St Petersburg, 1909

B.S.E. (*Bolshaya Sovetskaya Entsiklopediya*), 2nd ed., vol. 42, Moscow, 1942

BURYSHKIN, P. *Moskva kupecheskaya*, Chekhov Publications, New York, 1954

BUXHOEVEDEN, SOPHIE *The Life and Tragedy of Alexandra Feodorovna, Empress of Russia*, Longmans, Green & Co., London, 1928

CALVOCORESSI, M. D. *A Survey of Russian Music*, Penguin, London, 1945

Census 1897 (*Pervaya vseobshchaya perepis nasaleniya Rossiyskoy Imperii, proizvedennaya 28 yanvarya 1897 g.*)

CHELINTSEV, A. N. *Russkoye selskoye khozyaystvo pered revolyutsiyey*, 2nd ed., Moscow, 1928, quoting agricultural census of 1916

CHESHIKHIN, V. *Istoriya russkoy opery (s 1674 po 1903 g.)*, 2nd ed., St Petersburg, 1905

DARLINGTON, THOMAS 'Education in Russia', *Board of Education Special Reports on Educational Subjects*, vol. 23, London, 1909

DENIKE, YU. 'Kupecheskaya semya Tikhomirnovykh' in *Novy Zhurnal*, no. 68, June 1962, New York

DEUTSCH, LEV *Rol yevreyev v russkom revolyutsionnom dvizhenii*, Berlin, 1923

DIJUR, I. M. 'Jews in the Russian Economy' in *Russian Jewry (1860–1917)*, Ed. J. Frumkin, G. Aronson and A. Goldenweiser, Union of Russian Jews, Thomas Yoseloff, New York, 1966

DUBROVIN, N. F. 'Nashi mistiki-sektanty' in *Russkaya Starina*, no. 2 (February) 1896, St Petersburg, 1896

Encyclopaedia Britannica, 11th ed., vol. 3, London, 1910. Article: 'Ballet'

ETTINGER, S. 'The Jews in Russia at the Outbreak of the Revolution' in *The Jews in Russia since 1917*, Ed. L. Kochan, Institute of Jewish Affairs, Oxford University Press, 1970

FINN-ENOTAYEVSKY *Sovremennoye khozyaystvo v Rossii (1890–1910)*, St Petersburg, 1911

FLORINSKY, M. T. *Russia. A History and an Interpretation*, Macmillan, New York, 1964

GARTHOFF, R. E. 'The Military as a Social Force' in *The Transformation of Russian Society. Aspects of Social Change since 1861*, Ed. C. E. Black, Harvard University Press, 1960

GERSCHENKRON, ALEXANDER 'Problems of Russian Economic Development', in *The Transformation of Russian Society. Aspects of Social Change since 1861*, Ed. C. E. Black, Harvard University Press, 1960

GINSBURG, M. 'Art Collectors of Old Russia: The Morozovs and the Shchukins' in *Apollo*, December 1973, London

GORKI, MAXIM *Sobraniye sochineniy*, vol. 18, Moscow, 1963

GRAY, CAMILLA *The Great Experiment: Russian Art 1863–1922*, Thames & Hudson, London, 1962

GREENBERG, L. *The Jews in Russia*, Yale University Press, 1944

HANS, N. *History of Russian Educational Policy*, London, 1931

KAIDANOVA, OLGA *Ocherki po istorii narodnovo obrazovaniya v Rossii i SSSR na osnovye lichnovo opyta i nablyudeniy*, Part I, Berlin 1938, Part II, Brussels, 1939

KAMENSKY, VASILI *Put entusiasta. Avtobiograficheskaya kniga*, Perm, 1968

KARSAVINA, TAMARA *Theatre Street*, 2nd ed., Constable, London, 1948

KIZEVETTER, A. *Na rubezhe dvukh stoletiy. Vospominaniya 1881–1914*, Prague, 1929

KHROMOV, P. *Ekonomicheskoye razvitie Rossii v XIX i XX vekakh, 1800–1917*, Moscow, 1950

LENIN, V. I. *Polnoye sobraniye sochineniy*, 5th ed., vols 16 and 17, Moscow, 1961

LIEVEN, PETER *The Birth of Ballets-Russes*, Trans. L. Zarine, 2nd impression, Allen & Unwin, London, 1956

LUCKETT, R. *The White Generals. An Account of the White*

Movement and the Russian Civil War, Longman, London, 1971

MCCAULEY, M. *The Russian Revolution and the Soviet State, 1917–1921. Documents*, London, 1975

MASSIE, ROBERT *Nicholas and Alexandra*, Gollancz, London, 1968

MATCHENKO, I. *Obozreniye Rossiskoy Imperii sravnitelno s vazhneyshimi gosudarstvami*, 15th ed., Kiev, 1913

MICHAEL ALEXANDROVICH, GRAND-DUKE *Diary* (in Russian), part T/s, part M/s, unpublished, in private possession

MILYUKOV, P. *Ocherki iz istorii russkoy kultury*, Jubilee ed., Paris, 1931

MOSSOLOV, A. *At the Court of the Last Tsar*, London, 1961

NEMIROVICH-DANCHENKO, V. I. *Iz proshlovo*, Moscow, 1938

NICHOLAS II, EMPEROR *Dnevnik imperatora Nikolaya II, 1890–1906*, Berlin, 1923

NICHOLAS MIKHAILOVICH, GRAND-DUKE *Lettres inédites à Frédéric Masson (1914–1918)*. Published by the Bibliothèque slave de Paris as *La fin du tsarisme*, Payot, Paris, 1968

Novy entsiklopedichesky slovar, (A–O), Petrograd, 1916

PALMER, FRANCIS H. E. *Russian Life in Town and Country*, London, 1901

PAZHITNOV, K. A. *Polozheniye rabochevo klassa v Rossii*, St Petersburg, 1906

RABENECK, LEV 'Moskva i yeya "khozyayeva"', in *Vozrozhdeniye*, no. 105, Sept. 1960, Paris, pp. 101–3

RIASANOVSKY, N. V. *A History of Russia*, Oxford University Press, New York, 1963

ROMANOVSKY-KRASSINSKY, PRINCESS M. *Dancing in Petersburg. The Memoirs of Kschessinska*, Gollancz, London, 1960

ROOSA, RUTH A. 'Workers' Insurance Legislation and the Role of the Industrialists in the Period of the Third State Duma' in *The Russian Review*, vol. 34, no. 4, October 1975, New York

SCHAPIRO, LEONARD *The Communist Party of the Soviet Union*, Methuen, London, 1970

SETON-WATSON, H. *The Russian Empire, 1801–1917*, Oxford University Press, 1967

SLIOZBERG, G. B. *Dela minuvishikh dney: zapiski russkavo yevreya*, Paris, 1933

SLIOZBERG, G. B. *Dorevolyutsionniy stroy Rossii*, Paris, 1933

SOBOLEV, YU. *V. I. Nemirovich-Danchenko*, Petersburg, 1918

SOLOVIEV, V. *L'idée russe*, Paris, 1888

STANISLAVSKY, K. S. 'Moya zhizn v iskusstvye' in *Sobraniye sochineniy*, vol. 1, Moscow, 1954

TALBOT RICE, TAMARA *A Concise History of Russian Art*, Thames & Hudson, London, 1963

TIMASHEV, N. S. 'Overcoming Illiteracy: Public Education in Russia 1880–1940' in *The Russian Review*, vol. 2, no. 1, Autumn 1942, New York

VIROUBOVA, ANNA *Memories of the Russian Court*, Macmillan, New York, 1925

VORRES, IAN *The Last Grand-Duchess*, Hutchinson, London, 1964

WILLIAMS, H. W. *Russia of the Russians*, Pitman & Sons, London, 1914

YEVREYSKOYE STATISTICHESKOYE OBSHCHESTVO (Jewish Statistical Co.), *Yevreyskoye naseleniye Rossii po dannym perepisi 1897 g. i po noveyshim istochnikam*, Petrograd, 1917

ZAGORSKY, S. O. *State Control of Industry during the War*, Economic and Social History of the World War, Russian Series, Yale University Press, 1928

ZENKOVSKY, S. *Pan-Turkism and Islam in Russia*, Harvard University Press, 1960

ZERNOV, N. *The Russian Religious Renaissance of the Twentieth Century*, Darton, Longman & Todd, London, 1963

Imperial double-headed eagle,
inherited from the Byzantine empire,
in the Moscow Kremlin's Uspensky Cathedral,
the coronation church of the Tsars.
Of massive silver it commemorates
Peter the Great's rescue from the Turks.

Much of Nicholas II's early life was spent
as an officer among his fellows.
Here in 1890, still Tsarevich,
he is at table with officers
of His Majesty's Hussar Guards and, right,
his cousin the Grand Duke Nicholas Nikolayevich,
during the annual summer Guards camp
at Krasnoe Selo.

The Emperor's study in the Crimea —
bare enough except for the clutter of Fabergé frames
on the desk and the reproduction of an Alma-Tadema-ish lady
playing the lyre to another in a hammock.

June 1908, on board the imperial yacht in the Reval roadstead.
Nicholas II in the uniform of Colonel-in-Chief of the Scots Greys
and the Tsarevich Alexei, nearly four, await the arrival of Edward VII.

A corner of the Empress's apartments at Livadia, Crimea.
Ferns and massed lilies of the valley set off an impressive Art Nouveau nook
that may well have been ordered, like much of her furniture, from Maple's in London.
Her favourite colour was mauve.

The Empress Alexandra Feodorovna
painting poppy heads,
a faded snapshot by a court photographer.

74

The Empress, elegant and ill-at-ease with the Emir of Bokhara in the Crimea, autumn 1909.
Note the cameras on the table and the outsize thermometer.

The Grand Duchesses, Nicholas's daughters,
in the Crimea, spring 1912,
photographed by their aunt,
Grand Duchess Eleonore of Hesse.
Left to right, Marie, Tatiana, Anastasia, Olga.

*A naval band plays outside the Small Palace at Livadia
in the Crimea, the imperial family's late summer retreat.*

Saint Petersburg, from 1914 patriotically Petrograd, administrative capital of the Empire.
1914 population – 2,075,000. Its main artery the Nevsky Prospekt
then as now runs two and three-quarter miles from the Admiralty to the Alexander Nevsky monastery.
This view is wholly recognizable today. From the right: the Passage Theatre specializing in Russian operetta,
the dome of the eighteenth-century Armenian church and in the distance the globe-crowned
Art Nouveau Singer building – now a bookshop. On this side of the street
the tower of the City Hall and, nearer, the Bazaar or Gostiny Dvor,
a typically Russian development from an oriental souk; its 200 shops according to Baedeker
'less elegant' than the others in the Nevsky.

One of the capital's starred hotels —
the Hôtel d'Angleterre opposite St Isaac's Cathedral —
full board from 5 roubles (approx 10s 6d in 1914)

The Petersburg commissionaire
of the Azov-Don Commercial Bank.
His badges — 'Vive la France' and
'Russia welcomes her friends'
— celebrate President Poincaré's visit of July 1914.

St Petersburg: a view over the Admiralty roofs
          to the Peter I Square
with Falconet's Bronze Horseman just visible
     and the linked palaces of Senate and Holy Synod,
     eastward to the smoking chimneys
     of industry and the Gulf of Finland.

     A corner of the Cathedral
in the Fortress of SS Peter and Paul:
     icon-laden imperial sarcophagi,
          the entrance to the Imperial Chamber
     and a gigantic white porcelain stove.

The annual task of breaking the Neva's ice, 1911.
From the left, the baroque Winter Palace,
one of the Admiralty's exquisite neo-classical
end pavilions and more recent buildings
on the site of the Admiralty shipyards.

One of the last imperial funerals, 1908.
The catafalque of the Tsar's uncle,
Admiral-General Alexey Alexandrovich,
passes a bastion of the Peter and Paul Fortress.
In the background the Alexander (now Lenin's) Park,
apparently 'a favourite resort of the lower classes'.

The Director of the Imperial Bank,
     Nizhny Novgorod. His office is decorated and furnished
in a Russian version of 'Arts and Crafts'.

The mythology of Tsarist government offices is one
of sloth and obscurantism but this one,
     the Drawing Office of the Admiralty's Baltic Works,
          seems efficient enough,
down to the amazingly practical abacus.

A group of deputies to the Duma, the lower legislative chamber
     in the constitution granted after the Revolution of 1905.
Those shown here, judging by their dress, must be mainly of peasant origin.

St Petersburg interiors.
A masculine library in the Gagarin Palace
decorated in a Germanic Renaissance style,
presumably in the mid nineteenth century.
Right, *fin-de-siècle jungle*
in a successful photographer's flat.

St Petersburg's Vorontsov Palace housed
the Corps of Pages,
 the Empire's most exclusive military school.
Here in 1894 the Junior Class
 form couples for a dancing lesson.
The portraits are of Nicholas I and II.

Uniforms of the Corps of Pages:
left to right, guard duty in barracks,
 off-duty city uniform (seated), field uniform,
Kammer Page or page of the chamber
 on palace duty, Kammer Page off duty.

Countess Brassova (see opposite page)
took her title from an estate in the country, Brassovo.
Here is her sitting room, massed with plants, 1911.
The naive Empire style of armchairs and sofa is characteristic
of much nineteenth-century Russian furniture.

Furniture under dust covers
and minor old masters
in a country house near Moscow.

Countess Natalia Sergeyevna Brassova, née Sheremetevskaya,
the twice-divorced daughter of a Moscow lawyer,
and her future husband the Grand Duke Michael,
younger brother of the Emperor, at Gatchina, near St Petersburg, 27 June 1912.
The wreaths of daisies and the towering gateau are to celebrate her birthday.
The sad-eyed Countess is the ideal of Edwardian beauty.
The portrait shows the Grand Duke in seventeenth-century costume.

Karl von Meck, a Balt from Riga,
was one of Russia's railway tycoons.
His widow Nadezhda was
Tchaikovsky's patroness and correspondent,
though they never met.
These photographs of their vast estate
at Brailov in Bessarabia
in the south (sold before 1890) show
the scale of a millionaire's dependencies.
From the top: the mansion,
the village, the sugar factory,
the gates and beyond them the church.

*Tea, crochet and the newspaper
among the birch trees.*

*The old general, a veteran of the
Russo–Japanese war,
wears the Dundreary whiskers of his youth.
As often in Russia,
and indeed by school regulation,
his grandsons' heads are shaved
against vermin and the summer heat.*

*A toast at a luncheon party
given by N. N. Gordeyev, governor of the Tula province,
at his home, Yakshino.*

*A country coachman drives a kolyaska,
a low-slung carriage with a leather hood.*

The Easter meal. Note on the table, decorated with spring flowers,
the bowl of coloured eggs and the traditional Paskha (= Easter),
a rich cooked curd cheese set in a pyramidal mould and marked with a cross.

Little Princess Elizaveta Golitsyn has dinner with her governess on the Golitsyns' estate, Dolzhik, near Kharkov, 1894, watched by the housekeeper, laundress and maids.

All city-dwelling Russians who could afford it aimed at having a dacha, *or cottage, usually wooden, in the country nearby — they still do.*
Here is one near Moscow, on quite a grand scale, belonging to a wealthy French silk manufacturer; and, opposite, another, more modest, near St Petersburg.

All Russians gather mushrooms
in the woods.
Two boys, both from a cadet school,
mushroom-picking among
the pines at Sestroretsk,
a watering-place on
the Gulf of Finland.
The little basket
has a special name, lukoshko,
only used
for berries or mushrooms.

93

The pine-thatched field church of the Poltava Regiment, 1915.
The doors flanked by icons of Christ and St Nicholas
led only to the sanctuary, the congregation stood outside in the open.

Officer cadets
take the oath of allegiance to the Emperor.

Buriat soldiers of the Trans-Baikal Cossacks
surround the proud little son of one of their dignitaries.

94

Much of education was in military schools. Here, a mathematics class in the Nicholas Engineering School, housed in the Petersburg 'castle' of the murdered Tsar Paul I.

Military life has always involved tedious tasks. Making telegraph wires.

A cadet of the Nicholas Engineering School guards the regimental colours outside the guardroom at the Krasnoye Selo summer camp. The peasant-style fretwork was the main decorative theme of the camp.

Officers, December 1916. The one on the left wears a pilot's leather jacket.
The newspaper they are relaxing with, Russkoye Slovo *(The Russian Word), represented conservative views.*

Waiters and stacked cutlery,
tureens and linen
at the buffet of the
Constantine Artillery
School, 1907.

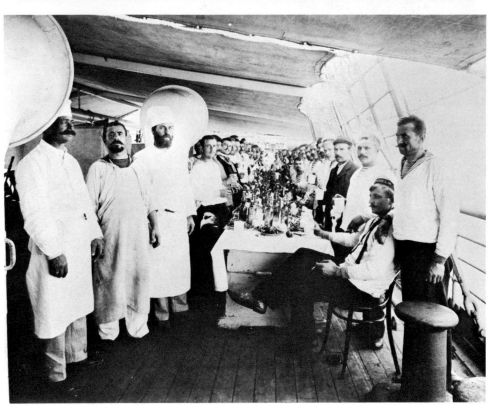

Drinks for crew and
cooks of the hospital
ship Oryol *(Eagle).*

*Men of the Guards
Horse Artillery undressing for
the banya (bath-house),* 191

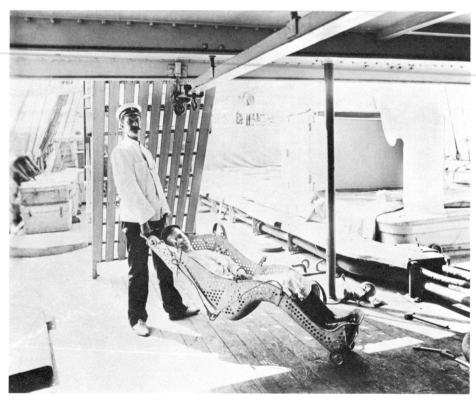

*An ingenious wheelchair
cum stretcher on the Oryol.*

The well-equipped operating theatre in a military hospital,
endowed by private generosity, Petersburg, 1914.

Military pomp. The nobly bearded
Grand Duke Michael Nikolayevich,
Viceroy of the Caucasus,
at the bicentenary celebrations of
the 18th Seversky Dragoons,
Tiflis, 1901.

Burnt-out buildings and
bayonets at the ready during
the 1905 Revolution, Moscow.

The Golden Company of Palace Grenadiers drawn from veterans provided the guard on monuments to emperors and within the palaces. Here, beset by curious children, in Moscow, 1910.

The modest rented house in Kiev of one of the greatest noble families in Russia.
The two cadets are from the Kiev Military School, after which they would qualify as officers.
In the background, the dvornik who kept the pavement clean and brought in wood for the stoves.

A shopping street in Kiev, capital of the Ukraine. The Mirage Theatre and a shop on the right
which advertises ladies' and gentlemen's hats, gramophones, musical instruments, English bicycles and typewriters . . .

Odessa, Russia's cosmopolitan main port on the Black Sea: here is its main street, the Nicholas Boulevard,
viewed from the City Hall, and Pushkin's bust in front of it. Below it on the right
are the harbours reached through the trees half way along the boulevard by the great granite steps
which form the setting for one of the most memorable scenes in the history of cinema, in Eisenstein's Battleship Potemkin.

*Two policemen, one from
      the country and one from the town.*

The Odessa fire brigade.

A furred Petersburg fireman sounds the alarm bell.
The notice gives differing signal patterns for day and night.

The larger cities were beginning to have public transport systems.
Here, horse-drawn trams in Moscow c. 1900.
By 1914 the tram system had been electrified.

1902, a Danish agriculturist's car,
one of the first in Siberia.
A peasant woman is said to have died
from a heart attack at the sight of it.
The chauffeur is letting it
cool off while getting lunch;
the owner has a sandwich.

A 'minibus' about to start on its journey in Omsk, Siberia,
its lady passengers with their motoring veils.

Railway stations: the platform at Karisalmi
in Finland and cabs waiting outside
the station at Vyatka (now Kirov).
As one might expect, Baedeker is a
mine of information on the railways:
take own soap, linen sheets
and air cushion; if you want a
compartment to yourself, buy four tickets.

The Baltic provinces had been part of the Empire
since the eighteenth century,
but to the eye were part of north-western Europe.
Here on Riga's waterfront,
fishwives and their customers.

A most tidy and un-Russian lock
on the Saima Canal,
connecting the lake of that name
with the Gulf of Vyborg above Petersburg.

A simple wooden chapel in a village
near Chudovo on the main Moscow-Petersburg line.

The imperial post ready to start from a remote spot, 1912.
Can this be the mail cart of which Baedeker warns:
'the passengers sitting on their trunks
or on the hay or straw with which the bottom of the cart
is littered . . . travelling is very rough and often painful.'

The slushy main street of Orenburg in Cossack country.
It can be taken as representative of many
provincial towns. Founded in 1735, moved twice more;
1914 population 94,000;
seat of a provincial governor and of a bishop;
35 Orthodox churches, one Lutheran, one R.C.,
14 mosques. In summer a band played daily on the
boulevard (view of the Ural river; restaurant).

Russian landscape at Odoev. River valley,
modest local Kremlin and a very bad road.

Jewish stallholders in a market in western Russia,
which had the greatest concentration of Jewish population.

Grünestrasse in the Lithuanian town of Kovno, 1917;
half its population was Jewish.
The ironmonger's shop advertises washstands,
baths and waterjugs.

A Jewish boy selling hazelnuts in Kutais, Caucasus.

Opposite, *the agricultural uses of camels: ploughing, central Asia; in winter near Samara.*

Above, *taking a polar bear on board ship in the Arctic Franz Josef Land.*
Bears, polar and brown, were commonly seen as rugs or stuffed and holding a tray for visiting cards.

The village of Slobodna, Tula,
south of Moscow, in August 1879,
comparatively recently built since
the trees are young and the cottages
and fences new. It must be pretty
much the setting of Turgenev's
Sportsman's Sketches.

Most Russian villages were built
on the simplest linear pattern —
two lines of cottages on either side
of a very unmade road, which with
the autumn rains and the dramatic annual
thaw of the snow (second photograph)
became a quagmire.

Peasants of the region of Oryol.
A genre photograph of the muzhik — strange hats and haircuts
and the typical duga or yoke used for harnessing horses.

In 1891 there was an appalling famine when the harvest failed in twenty-two provinces, leading to mass starvation. It provoked passionate comment from Tolstoy. There was a second severe famine in 1897. This and the following six photographs, which belonged to Constance Garnett, the pioneering translator of Russian literature, were taken during one of these famines in villages of the Buzuluk and Nikolayevsk districts near Samara on the Volga, in country with a large Muslim population. Above, a starving family.

Another family.

A woman gets her ration after two days without food.

*Father Smirnov, active in
organizing the supply of food.*

A charity inspection tour.

Tartars pray for help.

A meal provided by
the Samara Charitable Society.

A windmill, 1906.

A poorish wooden izba or peasant hut —
one room and the chimney
of a great stove/oven/bed.
Its owner in sheepskin tulup
and valenki, long winter felt boots.

A meeting of a mir, *the traditional peasant council*
made the basic unit of local government by the reforms of 1874.

Spinning in Estonia, 1900.

There was a growing interest in peasant crafts:
here, printing cotton from wood blocks in the north, 1906.
A photograph taken by the artist N. A. Shabunin
commissioned by the Alexander III Museum
in Petersburg to collect ethnographical material.

Women of Kakhetia in the Caucasus making bread.

СКЛАДЪ ЗЕМЛЕДѢЛЬЧЕСКИХЪ МАШИНЪ

МОСКОВСКІЙ НАРОДНЫЙ БАНКЪ
КОРРЕСПОНДЕНТЪ

ЕКАТЕРИНБУРГСКІЙ
СОЮЗЪ
ССУДО-СБЕРЕГАТЕЛЬНЫХЪ и КРЕДИТНЫХЪ ТОВАРИЩЕСТВЪ.

КОНТОРА и РЕДАКЦІЯ
ЖУРНАЛА
УРАЛЬСКОЕ ХОЗЯЙСТВО

АГЕНТЪ
СТРАХОВАГО ОБЩЕСТВА
ЯКОРЬ

СЕЛЬСКО-ХОЗЯЙСТВЕННЫЕ
ТОВАРЫ
и КУСТАРНЫЯ ИЗДѢЛІЯ.

This building in Yekaterinburg (now Sverdlovsk) in the Urals housed a depot of agricultural machinery, branches of the Moscow People's Bank and the Anchor Insurance Company, the editorial offices of Ural Economy, the Yekaterinburg Union of Savings and Credit Societies and a store for farming and cottage industry products.

An agricultural exhibition held by the cooperative in Omsk, Siberia.

*Haymaking in the Kherson province
of the Ukraine in the very south.
Note the southern* khata —
white-washed and thatched.

*Steam-powered threshing in Livland
(now Latvia), 1907.*

The Russian industrial revolution 'took off' in the 1880s and through the 1890s, and until 1914
the annual rate of growth was the highest in Europe. Much of the investment was foreign, both financial
and managerial, and the capital St Petersburg had its share in growth, mainly in the manufacturing sector,
and in foreign investment, about one fifth of all placed in Russia.
Construction began on No. 2 Mill of the British-owned Nevsky Cotton Mill on 29 April 1895.
It was spinning yarn on 31 December of that year.
The first photograph shows the laying of the foundation stone in June, accompanied by Orthodox ritual;
the second (opposite above) is a view of the incomplete building in October.

Workers of the Nevsky Cotton Mill. At the turn of the century 90 per cent of all urban workers
were classed as 'peasants' — many were new immigrants to the cities and industrial areas.
As late as 1910 ten per cent of Petersburg's population regularly went home for the harvest.

The founder of the Moscow
Fabrique de Soieries C.O. Giraud et Cie, with his sons and managers, 1891

Some of the Giraud silk workers with the ubiquitous country-style headscarves.

A Giraud workers' dormitory, Moscow, 1891.

Gold mine at Bodaibo in east Siberia, early 1900s.

The Transcaucasian oilfields near Baku on the Caspian had been opened up recently,
mainly with Swedish and English finance. The upper view to the distant wells
of Shibayev, Rothschild and Nobel is of 1899. A visit to the latter – in oldest clothes
and boots because of the pools of oil – was recommended as interesting. The Nobel company
maintained the petrol stations on the highways linking the capitals, Warsaw and Kiev.

The oil installations also had to be guarded against insurrection.

Below, a detachment of Cossacks in Baku during the troubles of 1905.

The Volga, longest of European rivers, runs 2305 miles
from the Valdai Hills near Tver
to Astrakhan on the Caspian Sea.
By its sheer size (at times three miles wide)
and its importance for commerce and for passenger traffic
it plays a large role in
the Russians' geographical consciousness of their country.
A voyage by Volga steamer was recommended
for pleasure as well as business.
Here are some steamers moored at Nizhny Novgorod,
chief trading centre of the river.

A priest reads a newspaper on a steamer.

Tolga monastery on the river near Yaroslavl,
founded in 1314 and rebuilt in 1609
after destruction by the Poles.
Its whitewashed walls, four churches
and belfry are the perfect 'holiday snap'
of Russian monasticism.
In front is a typical floating landing stage.

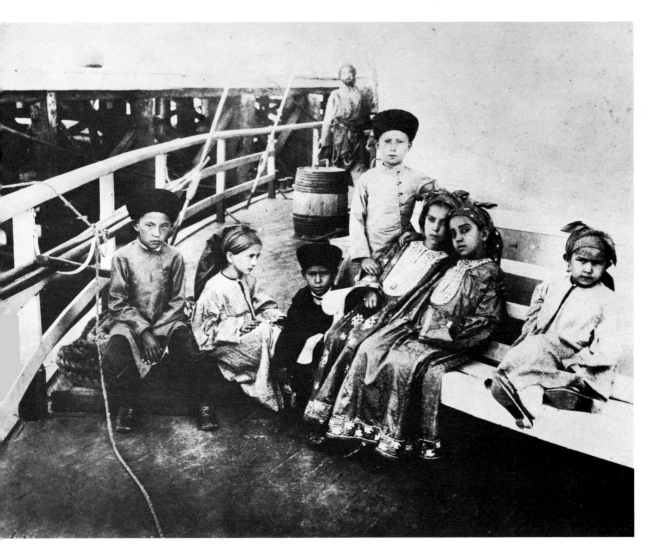

The Volga runs through the Tartar country of Kazan.
Here are Tartar children in traditional but one suspects not everyday costume.

A lumbering scene on the Volga.
The timber rafts were floated down the river.

Countess Karlova, morganatic wife of
Duke George of Mecklenburg-Strelitz,
a member of the imperial family
on his mother's side,
photographs boatmen and children
at Nizhny Novgorod, 1913.

Volga boatmen, a typical genre *photograph as sold to tourists.*

Nizhny Novgorod (now Gorki) lies at the junction of the Volga and Oka. The town's commanding position established
its commercial importance as did its summer Great Fair, copied perhaps from that of the Tartar Khans at Kazan.

The Fair lasted from 15 July to 10 September and was the largest of many thousands in Russia, indeed the world.
In Western Europe medieval fairs had disappeared with the coming of modern patterns of trade.

In Russia they remained widespread until the Revolution, though their importance waned with the coming of railways.
In 1910 the Nizhny Fair attracted 400,000 visitors and 250 million roubles' (approx. 25 million pounds')
worth of goods including tea, cottons, furs, iron, dried and salted fish, tanned hides, felt boots, Ural gems and oriental goods.

Opposite, the humbler area of the Fair. Below, Nizhny Novgorod viewed across the Oka from the Fair.

Bottom, the main Fair building, erected in 1890. During the period of the Fair
it housed a governor, Fair committee, police, and shops for luxury goods, and was surrounded
by a complete town of shops and warehouses, including four churches and a mosque.

A charming photograph of a Volga fairground stall.
It is probably somewhat earlier
in date than most of those in this book
and shows a junklover's dream mixture of old books,
saucepans, hammers, crockery, broken washstand surround
and what seems to be an edifying print of
the 'steps to Heaven and the steps to Hell'.

Pie seller on the Volga.

Moscow, 14 May 1894:
crowds and trophies strung with oil lamps
on Nicholas II's Coronation day.

Opekushin's colossal bronze statue
of Tsar Alexander III
near the Church of the Redeemer

Nicholas II's Coronation procession enters the city through the Triumphal Gate
and down the Tverskaya (now Gorki Street) running two miles south to the Red Square.
The carriages contain the Empress Alexandra and the Empress Dowager.

A classic view eastward up the Moskva river to the Kremlin, heart of the ancient and sacred capital of Russia.
The view is dominated, as it still is, by the Ivan the Great belfry,
its adjacent cluster of churches, of the Assumption, the Annunciation and the Archangel Michael,
and the bulky Great Kremlin Palace ringed by a wall of spires capped with eagles (now red stars).
Many of Moscow's 450 plus churches have since been destroyed. The block to the right of the Kremlin within the whitewashed wall
of the Kitaigorod or inner city is now largely occupied by the giant modern Hotel Rossiya.
But behind on the Red Square there still stands the fantastic St Basil's Cathedral celebrating Ivan the Terrible's
conquest of Kazan. Catherine II's Foundling Hospital (still extant) is on the extreme right.
Note the floating bathing establishments on the river.

The Upper Bazaar in Moscow in the 1880s. A development from pre-industrial and oriental trading habits, these extensive 'trading rows' were used for both retail and wholesale trade.

Winter on Kuznetsky Most (Smith's Bridge), one of Moscow's best shopping streets.
A police inspector strides proprietorially down the centre.

*The Moscow showroom of the famous jeweller Peter Carl Fabergé. The firm employed some 700 craftsmen and had other branches
in Petersburg, Odessa, Kiev (briefly) and London. Apart from the exquisitely ingenious imperial Easter eggs, the firm
executed official and private commissions of all kinds – a nephrite Buddha for the King of Siam, an icon for the Duchess of Norfolk,
models of the Sandringham farm animals for Queen Alexandra made of the unrivalled semiprecious stones of the Urals.
The stock included ordinary table silver and dinner services as visible here,
and all manner of enamelled and jewelled cigarette cases, bell pushes, frames and parasol handles.*

The stylish front and ...room of Kodak's Moscow branch, ...bably designed by George Walton and ...d on the Petrovka in April 1900.

A quiet view down the Yauza river,
a tributary of the Moskva
in the eastern part of the city.
The low, often wooden houses
and yards are still not
uncharacteristic of Moscow's suburbs.

A Moscow labour exchange — founded in 1915
in memory of the great Moscow industrialist Timofey Savvich Morozov.

The towered Vladimir or northern gate of the inner city wall.
It took its name from the church of St Vladimir (the smaller of the two)
built in 1691 to commemorate the deliverance of Russia from the Tartars.

Country fair at Panovo, province of Pskov, N.W. Russia,
at the entrance to Glubokoe, Count Peter Heyden's estate.

A fairground shooting range.

A picnic party in the Caucasus, 1910,
from the album of one of the many Englishmen
who worked in Russia, mainly as managers.

A chinoiserie roundabout in Siberia.

Officers of the Life Guards Artillery
brigade pose carefully at
cards and dominoes under a grand-ducal portrait
in their Petersburg mess.
Their refreshment appears to be glasses of tea.

Snooker. It might be Aldershot or Saumur
rather than the Guards Cossacks.

*The lighter side of the early days of war.
The Colonel of the 200th Regiment of Foot
plays the piano in occupied Galicia, 1914.*

*An officer of the Cossacks of the Imperial Guard
with his 'bag', 1907.*

The pearl-encrusted costume of a seventeenth century
boyaryshna, *an unmarried girl of the nobility: this was worn*
for the Winter Palace court ball of 22 January 1903
for which all present from the Tsar down wore costumes
of the period of Tsar Alexis.

Fancy dress dance in the house of Konstantin
Petrovich Bakhroushin, wealthy Moscow merchant
industrialist and patron of the theatre, 1913.
Left to right, Field-Marshal Prince Suvorov,
his sovereign Catherine the Great,
her bluestocking friend Princess Dashkova
and her grandson Tsar Alexander I.

Brothers and sisters in national fancy dress, Biarritz, 1913.
From the left, the costumes of Mordva, Oryol, Tula, and Russian shirts and boots.

A little girl under the eyes of two nyanyas *or nannies takes tea from her personal samovar.*

Princess E. Golitsyn, her governess and
two friends playing country tennis
at 'Dolzhik', province of Kharkov, 1906.

Anacleto Pasetti, St Petersburg
photographer, presses the bulb to take
his family gathered round the piano.

Russian family on Côte d'Azur beach, c. 1910.

The Crimea, once a Tartar Khanate,
has been Russian since 1783.

By 1900 the climate, its spectacular
mountains dropping to the sea and
lush greenery made it a second Riviera.

Yalta, scene of Chekhov's
Lady with a Little Dog, was the most
fashionable resort and adjoined the
imperial retreats at Livadia.

Here are a hotel at Gurzuf and villas
at Alupka, both on the sea near Yalta.

Biarritz, a fishing village in the Basque country,
had become fashionable throughout Europe with the Empress Eugénie,
then Edward VII and Mrs Keppel; and many wealthy Russians
wintered there. M. and Mme Staheyeff, from Moscow,
on the promenade along the Grande Plage, 1913.

Elegant ladies on the station platform of Gatchina,
a holiday resort near Petersburg.
Across the tracks the 3rd class buffet.

The lake on the von Mecks' estate on which Tchaikovsky would sometimes compose in a punt.

Motor racing on the Volkonsky Chausée near St Petersburg,
sponsored by Avtomobil magazine, c. 1910.

The fashionable crowd watching the manoeuvres
given for the French President Félix Faure at Krasnoe Selo, 1897.

In Orthodox churches the sanctuary is guarded by
*   the triple-doored iconostasis, an icon-covered screen.*
Only the priests can use the central tsarskiye doors.
*   This eighteenth-century screen stood in the chapel*
of a merchant family in Yekaterinburg (now Sverdlovsk).

The Virgin of Kazan, one of Russia's most revered icons, is borne in procession on 8 July, her feast day, from the lavra
or monastery of St Alexander Nevsky in Petersburg built to honour that saint's victory in 1242 over the Swedes
and Teutonic Knights. The icon was usually kept in Petersburg's Kazan Cathedral. Few people were aware that it was merely a copy.
The original (probably sixteenth century) was kept in a monastery in Kazan from where it was stolen in 1904.
It reappeared (and has been identified with a fair degree of certainty) in Western Europe after the Second World War.
It was eventually acquired by the Russian Orthodox Church in the U.S.A.

The funeral of some dignitary attended by many members of the higher clergy.
A cadet is carrying the deceased's icon in front of the coffin, closed after the service.

R.I.P. — a cemetery in winter.

*A bishop presiding perhaps over
the consecration of a church.
He is standing on a circular mat, orlets,
which is always placed
where a bishop might officiate.*

The higher clerics were drawn from the monastic 'black clergy'.
The 'white clergy' provided the parish priests who had to marry before ordination.
Here is a village priest, his wife and baby, 1902.

the woods near the Trinity and St Sergius lavra
lay the Gethsemane Skit or Hermitage. The monks
here are watering young trees by the church,
but some of their fellow hermits never left their cells.
Note the monk with keys who would
be in charge of food and the security of the library.

Monasteries were landowners (though much
of their wealth had been confiscated by
earlier Tsars) and monks had to work the land
like any peasant. These in sheepskin coats
and lapti are from near Nizhny Novgorod
(now Gorki) and are only
to be distinguished by their headdress.

Pilgrims -- in 1914 still over 100,000 a year
came down past this holy well to the walls of the lavra (monastery)
of the Trinity and St Sergius. The lavra in Zagorsk, 44 miles from Moscow,
was the richest and most historic of the Russian monasteries.
It is now the seat of the Patriarch and a seminary, and still houses the
massive silver tomb of St Sergius and a resplendent treasury.

The roads of Russia were tramped by many pilgrims
like these two, going from holy place to holy place
and subsisting on alms and monastic charity.

Many dreamt of the ultimate pilgrimage to the Holy Land,
the guardianship of whose shrines had formed the excuse for the Crimean War.
These peasant pilgrims are on their way from the Crimea to Jerusalem.

*Of all the myriad religious sects few excited more comment than the very small one
        of the Skoptsy; they saw women as the main obstacle to salvation and castrated themselves.
The most highly respected converts were those who joined the sect with a family.
On Russian territory they were to be found mainly in Bessarabia, since the majority lived in Rumania.
        To belong to the sect was a criminal offence involving deportation to eastern Siberia.
        However, the law was not applied very strictly. Here are ten of these sad eunuchs.*

A Tartar mosque on the Volga above Astrakhan.

A Kazan mullah and his wives. There were over 20 million Muslims in the Empire.

In 1864 all of Caucasia had finally been taken into the Empire; five years earlier
the Imam Shamil had been captured after more than two decades of holy war. The great natural beauty
of the mountains which divide Europe from Asia, and the diversity of the peoples of the Caucasus
inspired some of the finest Russian writers — Pushkin, Lermontov, Tolstoy.
Vladikavkaz, 'mistress of the Caucasus' (now Ordzhonikidze), took its name and importance from its position
at the entrance to the great Georgian Military Road to Tiflis. Here is the Alexandrovsky Prospekt,
the lime-fringed main street of the sleepy garrison town, looking south to the mountains.

Work on the Georgian military road in winter.

Tiflis, enclosed by the mountains, became capital of the Christian kingdom of Georgia in the sixth century.
Annexed by Russia in 1801, it was the seat of the Viceroy of the Caucasus.
The photograph shows the ruins of the castle built by the Persians, above some of the houses of the older quarter.
The trees are those of the botanical gardens.

Part of the bazaar
and a metalworker's shop, Tiflis.
The city was the trading centre for
the magnificent carpets and textiles
of the region.
Daggers and knives are much in evidence
— more for the tourist
than the Daghestan warrior.

The Caucasus — 'language mountain' to medieval Arabs — is astonishing in the diversity of its peoples:
Georgians with a long independent history, Circassians favoured by the Ottomans as slaves for their beauty,
ancient communities of Jews, Muslim tribesmen . . . Shown here: an officer of the Caucasian Cossacks
in full dress uniform and his much younger and pregnant wife;
an Armenian lady posed in the studio before a kelim; *Armenian cab-drivers in Tiflis, 1892; Tiflis wrestlers.*

The village of Adish (6690 ft) just south of the Central Caucasus range.
The watch towers attached to many of the houses date from the years of constant local fighting
— like the peel towers of northern Britain.

Another uncomfortable but
picturesque mountain village
photographed in 1897–8.

A feast in a dukhan, *a Caucasian tavern.*

*The sanctuary of Shah-i-Maidan and the first slopes
of the Altai mountain chain in Central Asia.*

Much of Siberia and Turkestan was roamed by pastoral nomads, notably the Mongolian Kirghiz
— their characteristic dwelling a yurta, a circular wooden framework covered with strips of felt.
Here: pitching camp, 1906, and herd of horses grazing; the exotically titled Ambar of Sarikol and Tumchis
posing for Captain J. B. Mackintosh, 1906;
and the interior of a yurta in the steppe near Omsk — note the brass bedsteads.

From the mid-1860s until the bloody defeat of the Turcomans in 1889 there was furious empire building
in Central Asia, the country of the Oxus and of Alexander the Great. By the end
Turkestan had a Governor General and the Emir of Bokhara was a dependent of the Tsar
(though the Emirate was only officially annexed by the USSR in 1924). Foreigners even in 1914
were only allowed to visit Turkestan by special permission and the Afghan frontier was closed.
Travellers were recommended a khaki suit, frequent changes of raw silk or wool underwear, a dress suit,
dust spectacles and an ample supply of biscuits, but no starched linen or weapons.
This photograph shows the Emir of Bokhara and his ministers.

*Siberia: families like this in front
of a miserable dwelling were supplemented by
Russian immigrants, exiles and all manner
of men brought by the Railway.*

*Some of the ancient Jewish community
of Bokhara in the
wadded robes of Central Asia.*

Kalmuck chieftain (zaysang) wearing Russian decoration and the St George sabre awarded for personal valour; his bodyguard (left) is in Cossack dress.

Transbaikalia, the country east of Lake Baikal opened by the Railway:
Buriats and their carrier-reindeer, c. 1914.
Bottom photograph: Maimachin, just over the Mongolian border. Maimachin and its Russian sister town
Kyakhta were built on the frontier c. 1870 to act as the centre for the tea caravans
between China and Russia. By 1914 when this photograph was taken that trade had dwindled in importance.

A hadj *who has made the Mecca pilgrimage*
instructs little Crimean Tartars in the Koran.

A Buriat school in the east of Siberia, 1882:
on the blackboard a proverb
to the effect of 'all's well that ends well'.

A Protestant pastor takes a class in Latvia.

An exhibition of books, wallcharts and materials
for primary schools in the Ural town of Perm.

A classroom in the Catherine Institute, 1912,
with the usual krasny ugol *('fair corner') of icons.*

A carpentry class in a primary school.

Headmistress, chaplain and girls.
The atmosphere of the group points more to a charitable institution
than to an ordinary school —
but the provenance of the photograph is not known.

Another institutka,
from the Odessa Institute for
Girls of Gentle Birth.

The most sought after secondary schools for girls were the Institutes (boarding schools) founded by various Empresses,
led by the Smolny and Catherine Institutes in Petersburg.
Here are Institute girls marshalled in their old fashioned uniform of frilled bonnet, cape, apron
and white gloves outside the Peterhof Palace to greet the French President, 1914.

Konstantin Korovin's set for act III of Reyer's opera, Salammbô, 1910.
The oriental setting is one of Symbolist splendour.

Ilya Repin (1844–1930) dominated Russian academic painting
with such canvases as 'Tsar Ivan IV with the body of his son'.
In 1914, he paints the portrait of the great bass Fyodor Chaliapine,
who in the photograph is attended by his oriental servant.
Chaliapine, born in a Kazan slum, had made his debut in 1894.

Chaliapine in the title role
of Massenet's opera Don Quichotte.

The Mariinsky Theatre, St Petersburg, 1896.
The ballet is The Awakening of Flora
by the great ballet-master Marius Petipa.
Solyannikov partners Julie Kshessinskaya,
sister of the more famous Mathilde,
mistress of Nicholas as Tsarevich.

Mlle Andrianova of the Imperial Ballet
— very much a pre-Diaghilev ballerina.

A scene from Tchaikovsky's Nutcracker *as performed
at the Mariinsky Theatre, Petersburg; choreography by Lev Ivanov.*

The Tiflis branch of His Master's Voice, c. 1914. English manager and oriental customers
in their multicoloured padded khalats (still the Russian word for dressing gown).
Frederick Tyler, the manager, was responsible for completing H.M.V.'s very representative catalogue of Georgian,
Armenian and Tartar songs and music, much of it recorded on location. He also recorded the very particular Chaliapine.

Amateur dramatics at a dacha.

Early November 1910 at the remote country railway station
of Astapovo where Tolstoy is dying.
A newsreel photograph of Countess Tolstoy at the window
of the room where her husband lies tended
by his followers who kept her away.
She wrote in her diary: 'November 7, Astapovo.
Leo Nikolayevich died at 6 this morning.
I was not allowed in until his last breath.
I was not allowed to say good-bye
to my husband. Cruel people.'
The tiny village was packed with
the family, police, clergy and
the world's press, photographers and cameramen.

Officers and nurses under the blossom, 17 May 1917,
soon after the February Revolution.